THE ULTIMATE
Wizarding
World
JOKE
BOOK

It's a Hoot!

Laugh-out-loud fun for
Harry Potter fans of all ages

JEREMY BROWN

TABLE OF CONTENTS

BONUS LAUGHS!

THE FUNNIEST CHARACTERS IN THE WIZARDING WORLD

THESE WITCHES AND WIZARDS CAN CONJURE COMEDY AS QUICKLY AS HARRY CAN PULL UP A PATRONUS.

THERE ARE PLENTY of grim, foreboding and downright scary people in the *Harry Potter* universe, from Voldemort to Snape to Vernon Dursley. But there are also plenty of characters who bring levity and laughs to the series. Here are 10 mirthful denizens of the Magical World who cast comedy spells throughout all of the *Potter* adventures.

Ron Weasley

AS HARRY'S FAITHFUL sidekick and first true friend, Ron often finds himself unwittingly thrust into the middle of the ongoing battle against Voldemort and the forces of wizarding darkness. Given his slightly fearful nature, this produces endless opportunities for comedic reactions as Ron finds himself facing some horrifying creature or deadly spell. But Ron's somewhat unlucky nature also provides ample material for comic relief. Whether it's receiving a public shaming courtesy of a Howler from his mother or being forced to wear secondhand robes to the Yule Ball, Ron's misfortune, and his subsequent reaction, is always good for a laugh—especially when accompanied by Rupert Grint's rubber-faced delivery in the films.

Fred & George Weasley

ALTHOUGH THEIR YOUNGER brother, Ron, is often an unwitting participant in their jokes, twins Fred and George actively court mirth and merriment, quite often at the expense of others. Whether it's tricking their mother into believing one twin is the other or attempting to fool the Goblet of Fire into believing they're old enough to compete in the Triwizard Tournament, Fred and George have no shortage of jokes, pranks and assorted mischief to unleash on their professors and peers. In the end, it's no surprise that they drop out of Hogwarts (in typically extravagant fashion) and go on to open a joke shop that becomes the toast of Diagon Alley.

Argus Filch

HOGWARTS'S LONG-SUFFERING CARETAKER Filch is perennially roaming the halls of the castle with his trusty feline, Mrs. Norris, in search of students who might have been breaking the rules. As a result of his menacing ways, combined with his inability to exert control over his environment, much of Filch's humor comes at his own expense. Many of his best moments come in the fifth book and movie, *Harry Potter and the Order of the Phoenix*. Aligning himself with new headmaster Dolores Umbridge (who shares his passion for punishment), Filch spends the majority of the story trying to catch the members of Dumbledore's Army, who are training in secret under his nose. This results in a number of comical moments, such as when Filch ingests a box of bewitched chocolates (courtesy of the Weasley twins) and breaks out in a ghastly case of hives.

Luna Lovegood

AT FIRST GLANCE, Luna Lovegood can seem a bit off-putting with her scandal-sheet tabloids and Nargle-detecting glasses, but once the reader (or viewer) spends more time with the character, they realize it's all just part of her charm. An eccentric Hogwarts student who joins the story later in the series, Luna's oddball nature ultimately makes her one of the most endearing and, at times, unintentionally hilarious characters in the *Potter* saga. From wearing a necklace made of butterbeer corks to constantly being on the lookout for invisible creatures, from Nargles to Wrackspurts, Luna Lovegood can always be counted on to bring a smile to *Potter* fans' faces, even if that smile is sometimes slightly confused.

Gilderoy Lockhart

ONE OF THE true, bona fide celebrities of the *Potter*-verse has an outsized ego to match his roster of (mostly fictional) accomplishments. With his outward charm and winning smile, Lockhart manages to bewitch many wizarding women, including Ginny Weasley. However, beneath that alluring exterior, Gilderoy is a total phony, as inept with a wand as he is adept with a one-liner. His bumbling results in the bones being removed from Harry's arm, a gaggle of Cornish pixies being unleashed on his class and, ultimately, removing his own memories when he tries to wipe Harry and Ron's minds. Sometimes, people getting what they justly deserve can be hilarious.

Hagrid

THE MASSIVE, BIG-HEARTED and lovable gamekeeper is Harry's first introduction to the world of wizardry, and right away we see Hagrid is not without his playful side. When Harry's odious keepers, the Dursleys, insult Hogwarts headmaster Albus Dumbledore, Hagrid retaliates by magically planting a pig's tail on their oafish son, Dudley. Hagrid's humor often comes inadvertently, from blurting out secrets and following up with "I should not have said that" to his ever-growing collection of magical (and dangerous) creatures. Hagrid may not be trying to be funny, but he always makes us laugh.

Seamus Finnegan

A FELLOW GRYFFINDOR FROM the start of Harry's time at Hogwarts, Seamus is an affable, easygoing schoolmate to Harry and Ron. Unfortunately, he isn't quite as gifted a wizard, at least at the outset. His early attempts at magic, including trying to turn water into rum and levitating a feather, often end with his spells backfiring and exploding right in his face. Luckily, he manages to turn his penchant for combustion into a positive, detonating the wooden bridge at Hogwarts to prevent Voldemort's army from entering the school grounds.

Neville Longbottom

M UCH OF THE humor surrounding Harry and Ron's herbology-loving Gryffindor mate comes at his expense. Clumsy, forgetful and often in his own way, Neville produces laughter as the butt of the joke. When he first arrives at Hogwarts, he interrupts Professor McGonagall by gleefully spotting his lost toad, Trevor, and later ends up being carried off by a rogue broom. Perhaps his funniest moment comes in the *Goblet of Fire* film when, after giving Harry Gillyweed to help him breathe underwater, he watches his friend dive into the lake but not surface. Panicked, he cries out, "Oh my God! I've killed Harry Potter!" Luckily, the Gillyweed works as expected, and Harry emerges unscathed. By the end of the series, Neville eventually sheds his hapless persona at the Battle of Hogwarts, when he kills Nagini with the Sword of Gryffindor.

Crabbe & Goyle

DRACO'S DIMWITTED ASSOCIATES Crabbe and Goyle are a pair of bullies whose association with Draco seems to be driven by whatever clout they can grab. Unfortunately, they continually find themselves undone by their own stupidity. Whether it's stuffing themselves with cakes baked with Sleeping Draught or attempting to disguise themselves as Dementors to try and frighten Harry, Crabbe and Goyle could always be counted on to do the dumbest, and inadvertently funniest, thing possible.

Arthur Weasley

IT WOULD APPEAR that, in the Weasley clan, humor is as genetic a trait as red hair and freckles. Much of the Weasley patriarch's funny moments come from his fascination with Muggle objects and culture. This leads to a particularly hilarious incident when Ron and Harry commandeer Arthur's Ford Anglia, a Muggle car that he had bewitched to fly. Arthur's fascination with everything from batteries to rubber ducks makes for some entertaining and hilarious exchanges throughout the series. His collection of plugs, for example, is a particular point of pride, despite the fact that he is as baffled by electricity as most Muggles are by magic.

Witches and Wizards

GRAB YOUR WAND, CLIMB ON YOUR BROOM, PEER INTO YOUR CRYSTAL BALL AND HAVE A LAUGH AT THESE WIZARDING JOKES THAT WILL MAKE YOU LAUGH AS SURELY AS *RICTUSEMPRA* WORKED ON MALFOY IN DUELING CLUB.

Why is Voldemort addicted to Twitter?

HE WANTS MORE FOLLOWERS.

★

Did you hear about the witch who lost her temper while riding her broom?

SHE FLEW OFF THE HANDLE.

★

Why did the witch dump the invisible man?

HE WASN'T ANYTHING TO LOOK AT.

★

What's another term for a wizard duel?

A STAFF MEETING.

Where do Death Eaters buy their supplies?

VOLDE-MART.

★

What's the fastest way to get expelled from Hogwarts?

CURSING IN CLASS.

★

Why did Crabbe and Goyle almost fail out of Hogwarts?

THEY COULDN'T SPELL.

★

How do wizards keep slim figures?

THEY WATCH THEIR POTION SIZE.

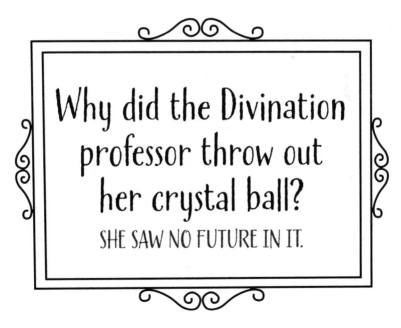

Why did the Divination professor throw out her crystal ball?

SHE SAW NO FUTURE IN IT.

Did you hear about the Hogwarts headmaster no one could understand?

They called him MUMBLE-DORE.

How about the headmaster who was terrible at football?

They called him FUMBLE-DORE.

Or the one who kept tripping over his robes?

They called him STUMBLE-DORE.

Did you hear about Albus's body-building second cousin?

His name is DUMBBELL-DORE.

A Muggle stepped out of his house one morning and looked up into the sky. Just then, Harry Potter flew by riding his Nimbus 2000. The Muggle stopped a moment, then walked back inside and picked up the phone. "Hello, police?" he said. **"I want to report a flying sorcerer."**

How do the Malfoys enter a room?
THEY SLITHER-IN.

★

What happens to a student who gets kicked out of Hogwarts?
THEY GET EX-SPELLED.

★

What is a bald wizard's favorite owl?
HEAD-WIG.

★

Why didn't the witch kiss the wizard after Potions class?
HE HAD BAT BREATH.

Why did the witches forfeit the baseball game?
ALL THEIR BATS FLEW AWAY.

What does Dumbledore hear when his doorbell rings?

A SORCERER'S TONE.

★

How many wizards does it take to cast a spell?

JUST ONE WILL DO THE TRICK.

★

What kind of dog did Dumbledore buy?

A LABRACADABRADOR.

★

How does Colin Creevey take clear pictures with his camera?

HE USES HOCUS FOCUS.

Why did Professor Trelawney change her email program?

HER CRYSTAL BALL TOLD HER "OUTLOOK NOT SO GOOD."

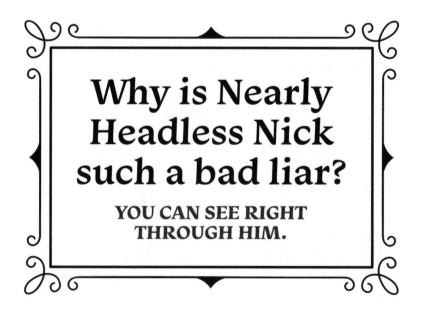

Why is Nearly Headless Nick such a bad liar?

YOU CAN SEE RIGHT THROUGH HIM.

What does Dumbledore use when he wants to speak with Snape?

SNAPECHAT.

Did you hear Hogwarts was opening a new school in Australia?

IT'S ONLY FOR WIZARDS OF OZ.

★

Why couldn't Voldemort order Nagini to rob Gringotts?

SHE WAS UNARMED.

★

Why did the Hogwarts professor turn his office walls to glass?

HE WANTED TO MAKE THINGS CLEAR.

★

Why was Voldemort unable to help Professor Quirrell?

HE WAS WRAPPED UP AT THE TIME.

Did you hear about the wizard couple who both drank Invisibility Potion?

THEY WANTED TO BE TRANSPARENT WITH EACH OTHER.

★

Did you hear about the hexed wizard who ate all the packages in the Hogwarts mail room?

HE WAS A TRUE PARCEL-MOUTH.

What do wizards drink on the train to school?

HOGWARTS ESPRESSO.

Why did Harry's godfather never laugh after the fifth book?

HE WAS DEAD SIRIUS.

★

How do you know you're talking to a pure-blood wizard?

WAIT FIVE MINUTES AND THEY'LL TELL YOU THEMSELVES.

★

Why is it so great to be a professional Quidditch player?

BECAUSE EVERY DAY IS FLY-DAY.

★

What's Professor Sprout's favorite drink?

ROOT BEER.

What's a good spell for a wizard who whose cauldron has gone cold?

EXPECTO PETROLEUM!

★

What happened to Barty Crouch Jr. when he drank too much Polyjuice?

IT MADE HIM MOODY.

How does Hagrid tell his pet gecko, Harry, what he is?
"YOU'RE A LIZARD, HARRY!"

★

Why doesn't Professor Trelawney own any books?
SHE ONLY READS TEA LEAVES.

★

What do you get when you bring Professor McGonagall to the beach?
A SAND-WITCH.

★

How can you recognize Voldemort's handwriting?
IT'S ALWAYS IN CURSE-IVE.

How did Dumbledore know Crabbe and Goyle were stealing candy from the Great Hall?
THEY HAD A FEW TWIX UP THEIR SLEEVES.

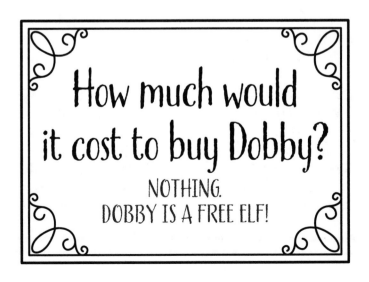

How much would it cost to buy Dobby?
NOTHING.
DOBBY IS A FREE ELF!

KNOCK KNOCK.
Who's there?
McGonagall.
McGonagall who?
**McGonagall call
my mom and tell
her I'm locked out!**

KNOCK KNOCK.
Who's there?
Sirius.
Sirius who?
**Sirius-ly, it's
cold out here!
Let me in!**

KNOCK KNOCK.
Who's there?
You know.
You know who?
**That's right, it's
Voldemort!**

KNOCK KNOCK.
Who's there?
Knight Bus.
Knight Bus who?
**It's night!
Buzz me in!**

KNOCK KNOCK.
Who's there?
He.
He who?
**He Who Must
Not Be Named!**

KNOCK KNOCK.
Who's there?
Wand.
Wand who?
**Wand-a open the
door already?**

KNOCK KNOCK.
Who's there?
Ron.
Ron who?
**Ron and hide!
Snatchers
are coming!**

KNOCK KNOCK.
Who's there?
Severus.
Severus who?
**Severus people
are waiting
out here!**

KNOCK KNOCK.
Who's there?
Quidditch.
Quidditch who?
**Quidditch asking
and let me in!**

KNOCK KNOCK.
Who's there?
Witch.
Witch who?
**Witch one of you
locked the door?**

KNOCK KNOCK.
Who's there?
Quirrell.
Quirrell who?
**I'll Quirrell with
you if you don't
let me in!**

KNOCK KNOCK.
Who's there?
Albus.
Albus who?
**Albus this door
down if you don't
let me in!**

**Did you know
Dumbledore drives
a magical car?**
IT CAN TURN INTO A DRIVEWAY.

★

**Why did Tom Riddle
leave Hogwarts?**
HE DIDN'T AGREE WITH
ITS MAIN PRINCIPAL.

★

**Did you hear
Ginny Weasley was
allergic to a Horcrux?**
SHE HAD AN INTOLERANCE TO DIARY.

★

**Why did the genie
turn the Slytherin
into a toad?**
HE JUST RUBBED HIM
THE WRONG WAY.

★

**What do you call a
polite Slytherin?**
A CIVIL SERPENT.

A Gryffindor, a Hufflepuff and a Slytherin are walking around Hogwarts when they come to a magical room they've never seen before. Inside the room is a slide with a sign next to it:

Climb on this slide and take a ride
Wish for where you'll land
Your wish is my command

The Gryffindor slides down, yelling "Chocolate!" And, at the bottom of the slide, a huge pool of chocolate appears.

Then the Hufflepuff slides down and says, "Whipped cream!" And she lands in a huge fluffy pile of whipped cream.

As the Slytherin gets ready to slide, his robe gets caught and he says, **"Oh, crap!"**

Good thing Colin Creevey had his camera when he saw the basilisk!

YOU SHUTTER TO THINK WHAT COULD HAVE HAPPENED.

★

What happened to Dolores Umbridge when she realized Harry had snuck into the Ministry of Magic?

SHE WAS STUPEFIED.

★

Why did Godric Gryffindor forge two swords?

HE THOUGHT THE FIRST ONE SMELT BAD.

What are a Slytherin's favorite magic words?

ABRADA-COBRA.

★

What does Sirius Black turn into during the holidays?

SANTA PAWS.

Why does Professor Lupin banish boggarts every morning?

HE LIKES TO EXORCISE BEFORE CLASS.

Why are the portraits at Hogwarts so lazy?
THEY JUST HANG AROUND ALL DAY.

★

What does Voldemort get from Nagini?
HUGS AND HISSES.

★

What kind of vaccination do you need to visit the Ministry of Magic?
A FLOO SHOT.

★

Why couldn't Jacob Kowalski start his bakery right away?
HE COULDN'T GET THE DOUGH.

Did you hear the Potions professor got a new pet?
HE WAS A SNAPE-GOAT.

Why couldn't the Muggle finish his book about Platform 9¾?

HE KEPT HITTING A WALL.

A Slytherin named Horace was searching around Hogwarts looking for treasure when he suddenly found an ancient lamp. He rubbed the lamp and a genie appeared.

"You have freed me from captivity, O Great One! For that, I shall grant you one wish!" Horace, who was incredibly greedy, knew exactly what to wish for.

"I wish to be rich!!" he said, laughing maniacally. "Rich, I say!!!" The genie nodded his head. "Very well," he said. **"Your wish is granted, Rich!"**

**Did you hear
Newt Scamander's next book
is a restaurant guide?**

*FANTASTIC FEASTS AND
WHERE TO FIND THEM.*

★

**Why did Voldemort team up
with Professor Quirrell?**

HE'D DO ANYTHING TO GET A HEAD.

★

**Why did Madam Pomfrey
see so many students right
before the summer?**

THEY WERE ALL SICK OF SCHOOL.

**What happened when
Professor Trelawney
broke her crystal ball?**

IT COST HER A FORTUNE.

★

**What does a wizard
roast at a campfire?**

HALLOW-WEENIES.

What happened
to Hermione after
she wiped her
parents' memories?

SHE BECAME THE LONE GRANGER.

A wizard accidentally turns his wife into a couch. He quickly takes her to St. Mungo's Hospital for Magical Maladies and Injuries.

He sits anxiously in the waiting room before a doctor eventually comes out. The wizard runs over and grabs her shoulders.

"Doctor, doctor!" he says. "Tell me! Is my wife OK?"

The doctor nods and says, **"She's comfortable."**

How should a Death Eater refer to Voldemort?

"HISSSS MAJESTY."

★

What do you call an alchemist with a bad cold?

NICOLAS PHLEGM-EL.

★

What do Professor Quirrell and Hogwarts have in common?

BOTH HAVE A HEAD-MASTER.

★

Why did Dumbledore let so many ghosts into Hogwarts?

HE LOVED TO SHOW SCHOOL SPIRIT.

What's Sirius's favorite historical event?

BLACK MONDAY.

★

What did Jacob Kowalski say when Queenie complimented his bread?

"THANKS, I KNEADED THAT."

Why did Dumbledore suddenly faint?

HE HAD A DIZZY SPELL.

A Spanish wizard arrived at Hogwarts to give a demonstration of his powers. He stood in the center of the Great Hall as all of the students sat to watch.

"I am Magnifico the Great!" he said. "And I am here to perform wonders that will dazzle and confound you! Witness now my first spell!!! Uno...dos..." **And then he vanished without a tres.**

**How do wizards
communicate with giants?**
THEY USE BIG WORDS.

★

**Did you hear about
the wizard who owned a
Thestral farm?**
HE HAD A TON OF NEIGH-BORS.

★

**What was the Heir of Slytherin's
favorite subject at school?**
HISS-TORY OF MAGIC.

★

**How could Karkaroff
afford the Durmstrang ship?**
HE GOT IT ON SAIL.

**How does Dumbledore
make a lemon drop?**
HE JUST LETS IT FALL.

★

**Why does Hagrid's chicken
coop have two doors?**
IF IT HAD MORE, IT WOULD
BE A CHICKEN SEDAN.

Which vegetable do
they never serve on
the Durmstrang ship?
LEEKS.

An absentminded Hufflepuff asked Professor Binns: In which of his duels was Emeric the Evil slain? Not pleased at being interrupted, Professor Binns's answer was simple: **"The last one."**

THE FUNNIEST MOMENTS FROM THE *HARRY POTTER* BOOKS

PUT DOWN YOUR REMOTE AND PICK UP ONE OF THE NOVELS TO INDULGE YOURSELF IN THESE HILARIOUS UNFILMED EXCHANGES.

AS GREAT AS the *Harry Potter* films are, they lose great swaths of story, subplot and characterization in the adaptation process. It's understandable, since some of the books top out at several hundred pages. However, that means a lot of classic moments were left on the cutting room floor. Check out just a few of these literary rib-ticklers that await you between the covers of the *Potter* books.

Snape Is Vexed by a Magic Pen

IN *HARRY POTTER* and the Half-Blood Prince, Snape becomes suspicious of the Potions book Harry has been using, which has allowed him to excel in Professor Slughorn's Potions class. Demanding to see Harry's book, Snape is perplexed when he opens it up to see that the book is not Harry's, but actually the property of "Roonil Wazlib." Thanks to a trick quill from Weasleys' Wizard Wheezes (more of whose gags can be found on pg. 82), Ron's name has been reworked into a nonsense moniker that puzzles even Snape. The situation is made even more absurd when Harry tries to convince the professor that Roonil Wazlib is actually his nickname.

McGonagall Offers Harry a Cookie

WHEN SENT TO McGonagall's office for detention after shouting at Umbridge and calling her a liar in *Harry Potter and the Order of the Phoenix*, Harry is expecting to be dressed down for his insubordination. Instead, McGonagall reads over Umbridge's note and then asks Harry if the report is true. When he confirms it is, McGonagall sits down and says, "Have a biscuit, Potter." It's a subtle gesture that shows Professor McGonagall silently supports Harry's rebellion, and also that she isn't without a sly sense of humor.

Dumbledore Is Amused by Lockhart's Fate

IN *HARRY POTTER* *and the Chamber of Secrets*, Gilderoy Lockhart is revealed to be a fraud when he confesses to erasing other wizards' memories and taking credit for their actions. He attempts to erase both Harry's and Ron's memories and claim to have saved Ginny Weasley from the titular chamber. However, the attempted charm backfires and Lockhart erases his own memory. Upon discovering this, Dumbledore seemingly takes great pleasure in the vain and egocentric Lockhart's comeuppance. He shakes his head in amusement and says, "Dear me. Impaled upon your own sword, Gilderoy!"

Fred and George Take Aim at Voldemort

YEARS BEFORE THEIR fateful encounter with the Dark Lord and his minions during the Battle of Hogwarts, it turns out Fred and George Weasley actually (and unknowingly) took a few shots at Voldemort. In *Harry Potter and the Sorcerer's Stone*, the Defense Against the Dark Arts teacher, Professor Quirrell, wore a turban on his head that smelled strongly of garlic. It made a tempting target for the Weasley twins, who pelted Quirrell with snowballs every chance they got. Little did they know that under the turban,  Quirrell was concealing the face of Voldemort himself, who could not yet take physical form but had possessed the professor. Of course, Fred and

George didn't know Voldemort was under the turban, otherwise they would have had sturdier ammunition than mere snowballs.

Custom Weasley Sweaters

IN THE MOVIES, Harry and Ron each receive a sweater with an "H" and an "R," respectively, knitted on the front. This is a subtle nod to another moment in the books, in which Fred and George receive the dreaded Molly Weasley sweaters. Never missing a chance to have fun at their mother's expense, they tease Mrs. Weasley, suggesting the initials on the sweater were so she could finally tell them apart.

Harry Zings Dudley

FORCED TO LIVE with his thoroughly unpleasant uncle, Vernon Dursley; his aunt, Petunia; and his spoiled glutton of a cousin, Dudley, Harry is often a hapless victim of their collective cruelty. But there are moments throughout the books that show Harry doesn't just take his punishment lying down. For example, in *Harry Potter and the Sorcerer's Stone*, Dudley paints a grim picture of life at Stonewall High, the secondary school Harry is due to be shipped off to before he is admitted to Hogwarts. He informs Harry it's standard practice for first-year students to have their heads jammed into the toilets as part of a hazing ritual. When Dudley gleefully suggests they go and practice, Harry declines, saying, "No, thanks. The poor toilet's never had anything as horrible as your head down it—it might be sick."

Hermione's Hats Go Missing

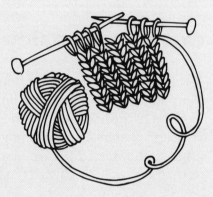

THE MOVIE ADAPTATION of *Harry Potter and the Goblet of Fire* eliminates an entire subplot in which Hermione strives for the rights of house-elves everywhere. That's a shame because it sets up some amusing moments, one of which sees Hermione knitting dozens of hats and leaving them around the Gryffindor common room. Her thinking is that the elves who clean Gryffindor house will take the hats and, having been given clothes, be freed. However, the elves are insulted by the gesture and refuse to clean Gryffindor, leaving the job to Dobby, who is already free. Hermione is shocked to discover the house-elf proudly walking around wearing all of her hats at once.

Dumbledore Takes the Dursleys to Task

ALBUS DUMBLEDORE HAS a few funny moments throughout the books that show his charming and somewhat silly side, particularly in the early installments. But it's in one of the later books, *Harry Potter and the Half-Blood Prince*, that Dumbledore puts his sharp wit to particularly good effect. Visiting Harry at the Dursleys' house, Dumbledore informs his guardians that Harry will soon be coming of age. During the conversation, he delivers a verbal beatdown to Harry's abusive family, telling them the one good thing they ever did was ensure he didn't grow up to be like their son, Dudley.

Ginny Spills a Little Ink

WHEN HARRY AND Ginny Weasley begin dating, a number of other Hogwarts girls start showing interest and pestering her with questions. One of the girls, Romilda Vane, continually asks Ginny if Harry has a Hippogriff tattoo across his chest. Ginny decides to play along, telling Romilda he actually has a dragon tattoo, specifically a Hungarian Horntail, as it is, in her words, "macho." In a playful twist, she adds her brother Ron has a tattoo of his own—a Pygmy Puff.

Dumbledore Goes Deaf

IN HARRY POTTER and the Goblet of Fire, muckraking journalist Rita Skeeter reveals Hagrid's hidden giant heritage to the public, causing a backlash that leads Hagrid into a depressed reclusiveness. Desperate to pull him out of his funk, Harry, Ron, Hermione and Dumbledore pay him a visit. During their intervention, Harry refers to Skeeter as a "cow" before realizing his headmaster is in the room. Apologizing for the breach of etiquette, Harry is met only by Dumbledore twiddling his thumbs and saying, "I have gone temporarily deaf and haven't any idea what you said, Harry."

Dragons, Magical Creatures & Magical Plants

READY FOR A LITTLE CREATURE COMEDY? SOME OF
THE MAGICAL WORLD'S BEASTS MIGHT DEVOUR YOU WHOLE,
BUT OTHERS WILL JUST SPLIT YOUR SIDES WITH LAUGHTER!

Charlie Weasley has a great story about Hungarian Horntails.
BUT HE DOESN'T WANT IT TO DRAG ON.

What was Hagrid hoping Buckbeak would do for the students in class?
PUT ON A TALON SHOW.

★

How did Harry free Dobby?
HE JUST SOCKED HIM.

★

What does a Hungarian Horntail like in her soup?
FIRECRACKERS.

★

Why don't dragons have breakfast?
THEY ONLY EAT KNIGHTS.

Why do dragons make terrible bosses?
THEY'RE TOO QUICK TO FIRE PEOPLE.

**Why didn't the fat
knight like to ride dragons?**
HE HATED GETTING ON SCALES.

★

**Which internet browser does
Dumbledore's phoenix use?**
FIRE-FAWKES.

★

**Did you hear Padfoot
swallowed a clock?**
HE GOT A BAD CASE OF TICKS.

★

**How does Hagrid
contact Aragog?**
ON THE WEB.

**Why does the porcupine always
win the House Cup?**
HE HAS THE MOST POINTS.

Why did the boy
Dementor fall in love
with the girl Dementor?
SHE TOOK HIS BREATH AWAY.

What was the first thing Professor Lupin ate after getting his teeth cleaned?

THE DENTIST.

What is Professor Lupin's least favorite day of the week?

MOON-DAY.

Did you hear Professor Lupin went missing?

HE TURNED INTO A WHERE-WOLF.

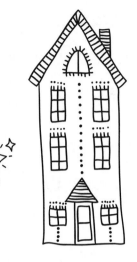

**Why did the mandrake
buy a house?**

HE WANTED TO PUT
DOWN SOME ROOTS.

**Why is Dobby
a good elf?**

HE HAS SO MUCH ELF-CONFIDENCE.

★

**Did you hear about the
grindylow's restaurant?**

IT'S A REAL DIVE.

★

**Why are basilisks
so handsome?**

BECAUSE THEY HAVE
LOOKS THAT KILL.

★

**I hear Gringotts
is doing really well.**

IT'S GOBLIN UP THE MONEY.

Why did Neville give Harry Gillyweed?

HE KNEW HE NEEDED SOME EXTRA KELP.

Why is Firenze no fun at parties?

HE ALWAYS HAS TO BE
THE CENTAUR OF ATTENTION.

Why did the centaur get kicked out of Hogwarts?

HE WAS HORSING AROUND IN CLASS.

Why couldn't the baby centaur talk?

HE WAS A
LITTLE HORSE.

KNOCK KNOCK.
Who's there?
Unicorn.
Unicorn who?
**Unicorn let me in
whenever you want!**

KNOCK KNOCK.
Who's there?
Who.
Who who?
**An owl!
Do you have a
letter for me?**

KNOCK KNOCK.
Who's there?
Veela.
Veela who?
**Veela you please
let me in?**

KNOCK KNOCK.
Who's there?
Dementor.
Dementor who?
**D'mean tor
lock me out?**

KNOCK KNOCK.
Who's there?
Fang.
Fang who?
**Fangs a lot for
locking me out!**

**Did you hear about
the party in the Owlery?**

IT WAS A REAL HOOT.

★

**What did the knight
get when the dragon
insulted him?**

A SICK BURN.

★

**What happened to
the knight when the dragons
threw a party for him?**

HE GOT ROASTED.

★

**How do you make
a grindylow laugh?**

TEN-TICKLES.

**Why did Madam Hooch want
the Whomping Willow to
join the Quidditch team?**

SHE THOUGHT IT WOULD
MAKE A GREAT BEATER.

Why wasn't the
underage ghost allowed
to visit the Hog's Head?

HE WAS TOO YOUNG TO BUY BOOS.

A dragon walks into the Hog's Head and heads to the bar. "Boy!" he says. "It's really hot in here!"

The bartender looks at him and says, **"Maybe you should close your mouth!"**

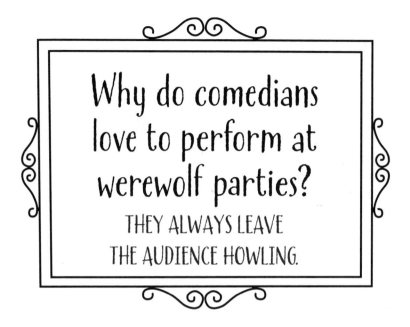

Why do comedians love to perform at werewolf parties?
THEY ALWAYS LEAVE THE AUDIENCE HOWLING.

Why did the Inferius go to bed early?
HE WAS DEAD TIRED.

★

Why is Grawp the most admired figure at Hogwarts?
EVEN DUMBLEDORE LOOKS UP TO HIM.

★

Did you hear Newt Scamander's pickpocketing pet had a cold?
NOW HE'S A SNIFFLER.

★

Did you hear Griphook broke his leg?
NOW HE'S A HOBBLIN' GOBLIN.

I heard that the ghost of a chicken is haunting Hogwarts.
IT'S A POULTRY-GEIST.

**Why did Lockhart need
a broom after his Defense
Against the Dark Arts class?**
TO CLEAN UP ALL THE PIXIE DUST.

★

**What does Nearly
Headless Nick like
to tell on Halloween?**
SCARY "LIVING PEOPLE" STORIES.

★

**Where would a
Chocolate Frog sit?**
ON A TOADSTOOL.

★

**What kind of coffee
does a vampire like?**
DE-COFFIN-ATED.

**What do zombies
do in the summer?**
STINK.

Why doesn't
Newt Scamander
drive a Corvette?
HE ALREADY HAS A THUNDERBIRD.

How did Voldemort save Wormtail's life?

WITH MOUTH-TO-MOUSE RESUSCITATION.

Did you hear about the rapping dragon?
HER RHYMES ARE FIRE.

★

Why does Buckbeak never study for exams?
HE LIKES TO WING IT.

★

Why don't you want a dragon to tell you a story?
THEY ALWAYS HAVE SUCH LONG TALES.

★

What do being a musician and being a dragon trainer have in common?
YOU HAVE TO KNOW YOUR SCALES.

How could you tell the villagers were excited for a visit from a dragon?

THEY WERE ALL FIRED UP.

★

What do you get when Fawkes visits Gringotts?

FLAME AND FORTUNE.

★

Why doesn't Nagini use any cutlery?

HER TONGUE IS ALREADY FORKED.

★

Why did Ron stop hanging out with the Devil's Snare?

THE RELATIONSHIP WAS TOO CONSTRICTING.

What is a grindylow's favorite wood?

WORMWOOD.

★

What do you get if you touch Fawkes?

A BIRD-DEGREE BURN.

What's the one room at Hogwarts where you won't find any ghosts?

THE LIVING ROOM.

Have you heard about the ghosts at Beauxbatons?

THEY GIVE STUDENTS THE CREPES.

What's the best way to talk to a dragon?
FROM FAR AWAY.

★

What happened to the Auror who had a tip on an Inferius in Diagon Alley?
IT TURNED OUT TO BE A DEAD END.

★

What's a fun game to play with a banshee?
HIDE AND SHRIEK.

★

Why did Professor Lupin cross the road?
HE WANTED TO EAT THE CHICKEN.

Why did Voldemort give Nagini a time-out?
SHE WAS VIPERACTIVE.

★

Did you hear there's a vampire professor at Hogwarts?
WHERE DID THEY DIG HIM UP?

**Why did the sea monster
have a stomachache?**
HE ATE TOO MANY POTATO SHIPS.

★

**What did one dragon
say to the other after
eating a comedian?**
"DOES THIS TASTE FUNNY TO YOU?"

★

**What is another good
name for Thestrals?**
NIGHT MARES.

★

**Why did the werewolf
leave Hogsmeade?**
HE WAS FED UP WITH PEOPLE.

**What do English
werewolves eat?**
FISH AND CHAPS.

★

**I heard Aragog was
working undercover
to help Hagrid.**
HE WAS A REAL SPY-DER.

★

**What do the spiders at
Beauxbatons eat?**
FRENCH FLIES.

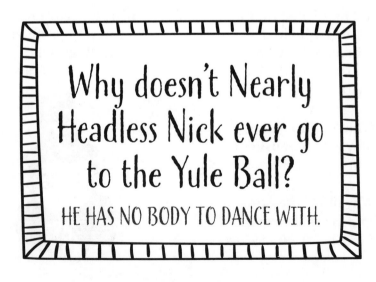

Why doesn't Nearly
Headless Nick ever go
to the Yule Ball?
HE HAS NO BODY TO DANCE WITH.

What does Sirius Black sleep in when he turns into Padfoot?

PAW-JAMAS.

What do you call a dragon that can't breathe fire?

WHATEVER YOU WANT TO.

★

Why is Professor Lupin such a fast eater?

HE ALWAYS WOLFS
EVERYTHING DOWN.

★

What's a dragon's favorite dinner?

YOU.

★

Why did the werewolf stop eating runners?

FAST FOOD ISN'T
GOOD FOR YOU.

Why is Mrs. Norris the best pet for Argus Filch?

BECAUSE SHE'S A REAL SOURPUSS.

★

How does Professor McGonagall turn into a cat?

PURR-FECTLY.

When Professor Lupin travels by plane, where does he sit?
IN FUR CLASS.

★

Is there a boggart that lives under an ottoman in the Gryffindor common room?
YES, HE'S UNDER A REST.

★

Why didn't Hagrid trust using grindylows in the Triwizard Tournament?
HE SMELLED SOMETHING FISHY ABOUT THEM.

I heard Newt Scamander had to take his Demiguise to the vet.
YES, HE'S IN THE OFFICE WAITING TO BE SEEN.

★

Why are centaurs so difficult to make plans with?
THEY SAY "NEIGH" TO EVERYTHING.

★

What is more impressive than Madame Maxime's flying horse?
PROFESSOR MCGONAGALL'S SPELLING BEE.

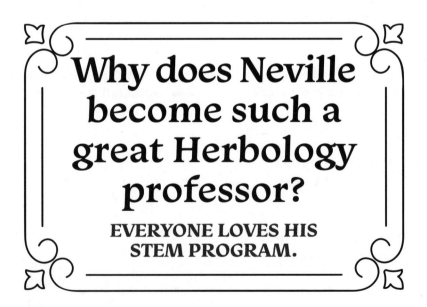

Why does Neville become such a great Herbology professor?

EVERYONE LOVES HIS STEM PROGRAM.

What do you call a unicorn
that can't get sick?

AN IMMUNICORN.

What do you call a unicorn that
gets covered in Stinksap?

A P.U.-NICORN.

Why are unicorns
useless in traffic?

THEIR HORNS DON'T WORK.

What
instrument does
a Beauxbatons
unicorn play?

THE FRENCH HORN.

What did the wyvern say to the knight?
"NICE GNAWING YOU!"

★

What is a Bowtruckle's favorite class?
TWIG-ONOMETRY.

★

What animal is impervious to Dementors?
A CHOCOLATE MOOSE.

★

How did MACUSA know Newt Scamander had smuggled creatures into New York?
IT WAS AN OPEN-AND-SHUT CASE.

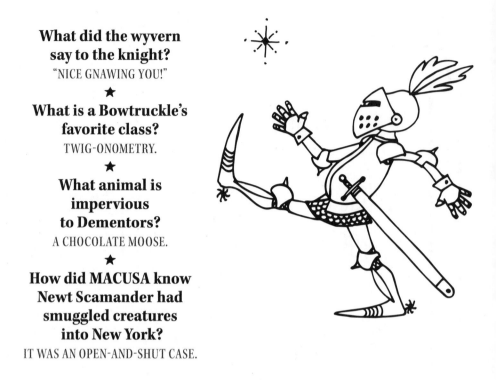

What time is it when an Erumpent goes to your house?

TIME TO GET A NEW HOUSE.

Have you heard a boggart tell a joke?

IT'S *RIDDIKULUS!*

**Why don't snakes
eat Slytherins?**
THEY TASTE AWFUL.

★

**What does a Fire Crab wear
when he gets dressed up?**
A BLAZER.

★

**Why does Mrs. Norris
at the beach remind
Argus Filch of Christmas?**
BOTH HAVE SANDY CLAWS.

★

**Why doesn't Newt Scamander
have a bank account?**
ALL HIS MONEY IS IN NIFFLERS.

THE FUNNIEST MOMENTS FROM THE *HARRY POTTER* FILMS

FROM LIQUID LUCK TO TAP-DANCING SPIDERS, THESE ARE THE TIMES WHEN THE WITCHES AND WIZARDS OF HOGWARTS CAST SMILES TO OUR FACES.

THE *HARRY POTTER* films can be magical, whimsical and even a little frightening at times. But all the movies have their share of comedy, from funny one-liners to outright hilarious pratfalls. Here are just a few moments from the films that lifted audiences' spirits.

Goyle Surprises Draco Malfoy

IN *HARRY POTTER* and the *Chamber of Secrets* (2002), Harry and Ron disguise themselves as Goyle and Crabbe, respectively, to try and infiltrate Slytherin House and uncover the mystery of the titular Chamber. However, Harry nearly blows their cover when he forgets to remove his glasses. Draco notices Goyle's eyewear and asks about it. Fumbling for an excuse, Harry (as Goyle), claims he was reading. Sounding genuinely impressed, and completely serious, Malfoy says, "I didn't know you could read."

Liquid Luck Hits Harry Hard

WHILE TRYING TO retrieve a memory from Professor Slughorn in *Harry Potter and the Half-Blood Prince* (2009), Harry takes a nip of Felix Felicis, a potion also known as liquid luck, to increase his chances of success. The potion has a surprising side effect, in that it makes Harry almost unexpectedly giddy. Overflowing with good fortune, Harry can hardly contain his good humor, as evidenced by his somewhat out-of-character performance during the funeral of Aragog, the giant spider who almost ate him during his second year. When Hagrid comments that people were afraid of his arachnid friend because of his eight eyes, Harry notes, "Not to mention the pincers," before making pincer motions with his hand. Although somewhat puzzled by Harry's remark, Hagrid finds it hard to disagree.

Ron's Traumatic Nightmare

DURING *HARRY POTTER and the Chamber of Secrets* (2002), Ron and Harry are almost devoured by a host of spiders residing in the Forbidden Forest. Although they escaped that particular dilemma, the memory obviously still remained in Ron's mind, as evidenced by his night terrors during *Harry Potter and the Prisoner of Azkaban* (2004). While Harry is poring over the Marauder's Map late at night, Ron suddenly wakes up in a cold sweat, shrieking "The spiders! They want me to tap dance!" Unfazed, or perhaps just used to Ron's arachnophobia, Harry simply tells his friend, "You tell those spiders, Ron!"

Fred and George Make a Fool of Umbridge

ONE OF THE vilest antagonists in the entire series, Dolores Umbridge takes great pleasure in making everyone's lives at Hogwarts as miserable as possible. No one, from students to professors and staff, is safe from her wrath, which is why it's so satisfying to see her finally receive a little payback. When Fred and George decide to leave Hogwarts for good, they do it with a bang, flying through the Great Hall and setting off fireworks. The last of these turns into a massive dragon, which chases a frightened Umbridge through the Hall before  destroying all of the rules she had tacked up during the year. It's a victory for the Weasleys and for Hogwarts as a whole.

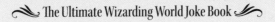
Draco Takes a Punch

AFTER TWO STRAIGHT years of bullying Harry, Ron and Hermione (not to mention everyone else in his path), Draco Malfoy finally gets a little taste of his own medicine in *Harry Potter and the Prisoner of Azkaban* (2004). After Malfoy gloats to the three of them over the impending execution of Buckbeak, Hagrid's Hippogriff, Hermione pulls out her wand but then thinks better of it. As she turns away, however, she decides to lash out with a swift punch to the face. Malfoy scuttles away and Hermione smiles, saying, "That felt good!"

Ron's Formal Dress Is Not His Best

IN *HARRY POTTER and the Goblet of Fire* (2005), Hogwarts students are eagerly anticipating the upcoming Yule Ball, which requires formal attire. For most of the students, this isn't much of a problem. But when Ron receives a package from the Burrow, he realizes he's in deep trouble. The robes he receives are a hideous purple color trimmed with white lace ruffles. Looking at himself in the mirror, Ron sums up his misery in three simple words, "Murder me, Harry."

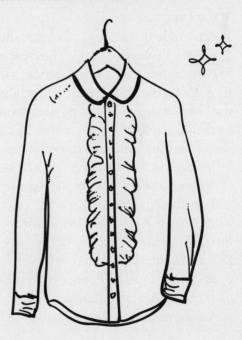

Hermione States Her Priorities

IN *HARRY POTTER and the Sorcerer's Stone* (2001), Ron, Harry and Hermione have a run-in with Fluffy, Hagrid's three-headed dog. After barely escaping with their limbs intact, the three of them return to Gryffindor and Hermione scolds both boys for their recklessness, telling them, "I'm going to bed before either of you come up with another clever idea to get us killed. Or worse, expelled!" After she slams the door, Ron gives Harry a look and says, "She needs to sort out her priorities!"

Facing Their Fears

IN *HARRY POTTER and the Prisoner of Azkaban* (2004), Gryffindor's third-year students confront a boggart during Defense Against the Dark Arts class with Professor Lupin. The creature, which lives in dark, enclosed spaces like cupboards and wardrobes, takes the form of each student's worst fear in turn. Using the spell taught to them by Lupin, the students are able to turn the boggart into much more comical shapes. For Ron, the boggart takes the form of a giant spider, a fear that Ron assuages by imagining eight roller skates for the creature's legs—no longer menacing, the clumsy arachnid can be laughed at, which can eventually banish the boggart. Next, Parvati Patil encounters the creature in the form of a giant cobra, which she turns into a jack-in-the-box. But perhaps the most memorable boggart moment comes when Neville steps up to the wardrobe and is confronted with Professor Snape in all his menacing, imposingly monochrome glory. Lupin, to whom Snape is hardly as frightening, suggests a surreal juxtaposition, putting the dour, simply dressed Potions master in the vibrant, eye-catchingly eccentric garb of Neville's grandmother. Alan Rickman's stone-faced delivery in the scene allows him to show his range in hilarious fashion.

McGonagall Gets Her Wish

PREPARING FOR THE Battle of Hogwarts in *Harry Potter and the Deathly Hallows: Part 2* (2011), Professor McGonagall uses a spell to bring an army of statues to life. As the massive stone warriors march off to defend the school, the usually stalwart McGonagall looks positively giddy. Giggling like a kid to Molly Weasley, McGonagall says with a wide grin, "I've always wanted to use that spell!" It's a nice moment of levity amidst the series darkest chapter.

McGonagall Poses a Valid Question

AFTER KATIE BELL is victimized by a cursed necklace in Hogsmeade, Harry, Ron and Hermione are summoned to Professor McGonagall's office. Looking at the three students, McGonagall says, "Why is it when something happens, it is always you three?" In response, Ron can only say what we're all thinking, "Believe me, Professor. I've been asking myself the same question for six years."

Spells and Potions

GET READY TO CAST A CHARM FOR ACHING RIBS.
THERE'S NOTHING UNFORGIVABLE ABOUT THESE
SPELLS, EXCEPT HOW HILARIOUS THEY ARE!

What's a potion maker's favorite baseball team?

THE BREWERS.

How do wizards diet?

THEY WATCH THEIR POTION SIZE.

★

What did the wizard ask his students when he tested out his invisibility potion?

"AM I MAKING MYSELF CLEAR?"

★

What did Professor Sprout say when Crabbe and Goyle were late because they overslept?

YOU SLEEP IN YOUR DORMS TOO?!

★

What does Mad-Eye Moody keep around his house?

DE-FENCE AGAINST THE DARK ARTS.

Did you hear about the potion made from pig ears and toad legs?

IT GIVES YOU HOG WARTS.

Why did Snape give up herbology for potions?
HE WAS NEVER THE SAME AFTER HIS LILY DIED.

★

What's the best coffee to keep Dementors away?
ESPRESSO PATRONUM.

★

Why can't anyone find Dumbledore's spell book?
HE KEEPS IT UNDER WARLOCK AND KEY.

★

What's the best spell for making guacamole?
AVOCADO KEDAVRA.

What's a good potion for poison ivy?
QUIT-ITCH.

What is the hottest boy band in the magical world?

WAND DIRECTION.

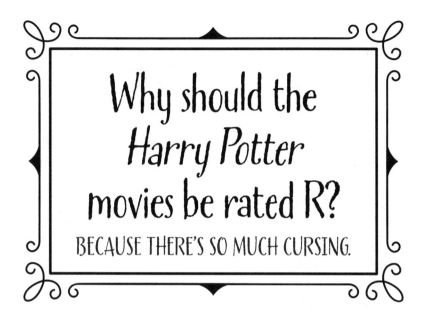

Why should the *Harry Potter* movies be rated R?

BECAUSE THERE'S SO MUCH CURSING.

What does Hagrid give to his pet parrot when she's thirsty?
POLLY-JUICE.

What is a Hawaiian wizard's favorite spell?
ALOHA-MORA.

★

What does Voldemort wear when he wants comfortable shoes?
HOR-CROCS.

★

Why did Neville get an F on his Charms essay?
TOO MANY SPELLING ERRORS.

★

Is Voldemort really evil?
OF CURSE HE IS.

**When is it time to
get rid of a potion?**

WHEN IT'S PAST ITS
HEX-PIRATION DATE.

**What happened when
the head of Slytherin took
a multiplying potion?**

HE TOOK ON SEVERAL SNAPES.

★

**Why didn't Ron like
Polyjuice Potion?**

IT MADE HIM CRABBE-Y.

★

**How long does it take
to cast the Levitation Charm?**

THERE'S NO WEIGHT.

★

**Why is it so hard to select a
course of study at Hogwarts?**

STUDENTS DON'T KNOW
WHICH CRAFT TO CHOOSE.

Why didn't Harry think he needed Felix Felicis after breakfast?

**HE'D ALREADY HAD
LUCKY CHARMS.**

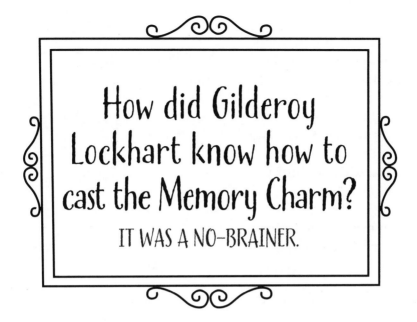

How did Gilderoy Lockhart know how to cast the Memory Charm?

IT WAS A NO-BRAINER.

Why was Dumbledore such a good wizard?
HE HAD A KEEN
SENSE OF SPELL.

★

What do Slytherin students get on their papers?
DARK MARKS.

★

What did Voldemort say when he used an invisibility potion on himself?
"IF MY FOLLOWERS
COULD SEE NOW!"

How do you unlock Madam Pomfrey's Skele-Gro cabinet?
WITH A SKELETON KEY.

What class at Hogwarts teaches how to make the best condiments?
SAUCERY.

★

When Professor McGonagall first decided to turn into a cat, what did she think?
THE IDEA GAVE HER PAWS.

★

What does Dumbledore do when he's tired?
HE RESTS FOR A SPELL.

★

What spell should Harry, Ron and Hermione have used against Fluffy?
EXPELLIAR-MUTT.

What does a wizard do when he wants to get in shape?
HEX-ERCISES.

What keeps a Hogwarts student's breath fresh?
ENCHANT-MINTS.

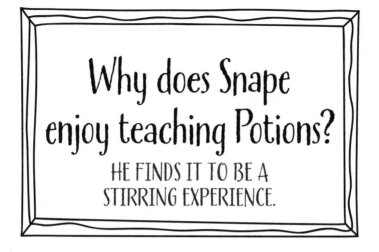

Why does Snape enjoy teaching Potions?

HE FINDS IT TO BE A STIRRING EXPERIENCE.

And what does a wizard ride for exercise?
A SPELL-OTON BIKE.

★

What do Death Eaters love to eat?
HEX-ICAN FOOD.

★

What did Hagrid say after Harry drank a Polyjuice Potion made with iguana scales?
"YOU'RE A LIZARD, HARRY!"

★

Have you heard about the new unforgivable breakfast cereal?
THEY'RE CALLED CRUCI-O'S.

In which class do you learn *Lumos*?
GLOW AND TELL.

★

Why did Snape go cross-eyed?
HE COULDN'T CONTROL HIS PUPILS.

I heard there was
a plan to make the Sword
of Gryffindor invisible.
BUT NO ONE SAW THE POINT.

★

How did Neville
do during the
levitation lesson?
HE DROPPED OUT.

★

What spell casts a Patronus
that's fine but not great?
ACCEPTABLE PATRONUM.

★

Did you hear Hermione's
Patronus was going
to take the shape of one
of her best friends?
SHE HAD TO CHOOSE
BETWEEN RON OR THE OTTER.

How can you cast
the perfect *Incendio* spell?
IT HELPS IF YOU WARM UP FIRST.

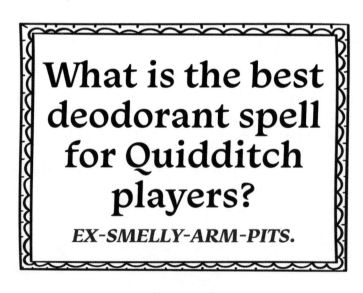

What is the best deodorant spell for Quidditch players?

EX-SMELLY-ARM-PITS.

Why was Wormtail such a good Potions assistant to Voldemort?

HE WAS ALWAYS WILLING TO LEND A HAND.

Where does Peter Pettigrew shop after aiding Voldemort's resurrection potion?

AT A SECOND HAND STORE.

Why wouldn't *Expelliarmus* work on Peter Pettigrew?

VOLDEMORT ALREADY DIS-ARMED HIM.

Why did Snape and Lily have the same Patronus?

BECAUSE HE FAWNED OVER HER.

Why was Snape so attached to his Patronus?

BECAUSE IT WAS DEER TO HIM.

Where does Madame Pomfrey cure invisibility spells gone wrong?

IN THE ICU.

★

What happened when Dumbledore felt dizzy?

HE HAD A FAINTING SPELL.

★

I wasn't always a fan of *Engorgio*…

…BUT IT'S GROWING ON ME.

★

What's the best way to keep all your potions safe?

WITH A WAR-LOCK.

What's another name for a freezing charm?

A COLD SPELL.

★

Why couldn't Snape use lacewing flies in his potion?

THEY WERE PAST THEIR SPELL-BY DATE.

How did everyone know that Snape had bad breath?

HE CAST A SMELL.

Even if you aren't a wizard, what are two magic words that will always open doors in your life?

"PUSH" AND "PULL."

What happened when the Dark wizards attacked the Quidditch World Cup?

THE FIRE WAS IN TENTS.

★

Why was Draco so embarrassed about *Sectumsempra*?

IT MADE HIM LOOK LIKE A BLOODY FOOL.

★

How did the wand feel after Harry cast *Nox*?

DE-LIGHTED.

Where can you find magical cows?

ON A SUMMONING FARM.

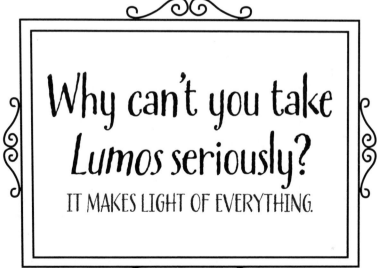

Why can't you take *Lumos* seriously?

IT MAKES LIGHT OF EVERYTHING.

KNOCK KNOCK.
Who's there?
Obliviate.
Obliviate who?
Hey! The spell worked!

KNOCK KNOCK.
Who's there?
Rita.
Rita who?
Rita Marauder's Map if you want to sneak out of Hogwarts.

KNOCK KNOCK.
Who's there?
Accio.
Accio who?
***Accio* locked the door again.**

KNOCK KNOCK.
Who's there?
Wand.
Wand who?
Wand-ering if you'll let me in.

KNOCK KNOCK.
Who's there?
Apparate.
Apparate who?
Apparate the doorknob and let me in.

KNOCK KNOCK.
Who's there?
Mrs. Figg.
Mrs. Figg who?
Mrs. Figg-s the doorbell, why do you think I knocked?

How does Peter Pettigrew feel about helping Voldemort?

SOMETHING FEELS OFF,
BUT HE CAN'T PUT HIS FINGER ON IT.

★

Why did Nagini bite Voldemort's shoe?

SHE WANTED A PIECE OF HIS SOLE.

★

Was Neville scared of Harry, Ron and Hermione when he tried to stop them from finding the Sorcerer's Stone?

NOT AT FIRST, BUT ULTIMATELY,
HE WAS PETRIFIED.

Why do good wizards never perform the Cruciatus Curse?

IT'S A REAL PAIN.

**Did you hear about
the new orthodontics
charm Madame Pomfrey
has been testing?**

BRACE YOURSELF.

★

**I hear Snape has a
potion for shyness,
but no one can find it.**

IT'S ALWAYS HIDING
BEHIND THE OTHER POTIONS.

★

**Did you hear about
the new wizarding
world fad diet?**

ALL THE MEALS ARE
POTION-CONTROLLED.

The staff at the
Leaky Cauldron just got
a new cleaning potion.
IT'S CALLED BROOM SERVICE.

Did you hear about the new textbook on levitation charms?

YOU CAN'T PUT IT DOWN!

Did you hear Hermione invented a powerful explosion spell?

IT COMES HIGHLY WRECK-OMENDED.

★

What happened to Snape when he drank too much invisibility potion?

HE'S STILL IN THE HOSPITAL WING WAITING TO BE SEEN.

WEASLEYS' WIZARD WHEEZES: A SHOPPER'S GUIDE

IF YOU'RE LOOKING TO MANAGE SOME MISCHIEF, HERE ARE A FEW ITEMS YOU CAN ADD TO YOUR CAULDRON.

IN THE HEART of Diagon Alley is one of the magical world's most prominent and popular stores, Weasleys' Wizard Wheezes. A joke shop founded by Fred and George following their voluntary expulsion from Hogwarts, the store began as a mail-order service before becoming the brick-and-mortar center of the Weasleys' comedy empire. If you're ever in the neighborhood, you might want to look into these items, whether you want to fake an illness or take on a Dark wizard.

Skiving Snackboxes

PERHAPS THE CROWN jewel of the Weasleys' prank inventory, the Skiving Snackbox offers a range of sweets designed to make the eater develop a variety of symptoms, all with the goal of keeping them out of class. Two of the most popular items are Puking Pastilles and Fainting Fancies. These snackboxes rocket to popularity during *Harry Potter and the Order of the Phoenix* when Fred and George sell them to students looking to skip Dolores Umbridge's Defense Against the Dark Arts class. Once the brothers go into business for themselves, the snackboxes become a staple of their inventory.

Extendable Ears

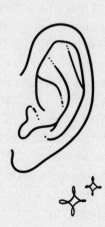

A HANDY DEVICE INVENTED by the Weasley twins as a means of hearing what the Order of the Phoenix was up to, Extendable Ears look, and function, just like actual ears. The only difference is, they're attached to a string, meaning they can be lowered anywhere the listener wants, allowing them to eavesdrop and gather whatever information they're after. Very helpful for uncovering the secrets of plotting wizards or just finding out what your parents are up to without them knowing about it.

Portable Swamps

DURING THEIR ONGOING war against headmistress Dolores Umbridge in *Harry Potter and the Order of the Phoenix*, Fred and George plant one of these items near her office, causing an actual swamp to sprout up around the halls of Hogwarts. Before departing the school for good, Fred and George use the success of the Portable Swamp as the perfect advertising vehicle for Weasleys' Wizard Wheezes, which they plan to open in Diagon Alley. It's hard to argue with that kind of success.

Decoy Detonators

A PRANK ITEM THAT also proves handy in the fight against Voldemort, Decoy Detonators are objects that create a loud bang and emit black smoke, a distraction that allows the prankster to slip away unnoticed. For his financial assistance in getting Weasleys' Wizard Wheezes off the ground, Harry is given a bunch of Detonators as a thank you. They come in handy during *Harry Potter and the Deathly Hallows* when Harry breaks into the Ministry of Magic, using the Detonators to distract Ministry employees while trying to steal one of Voldemort's Horcruxes.

Edible Dark Marks

NO ONE WANTS to wear the Dark Mark, the universal sign of allegiance to Voldemort, on their skin. Unless, of course, that Dark Mark is one of these confections created by Fred and George. The taste isn't especially pleasant (the candies are even marketed with the tagline, "They'll Make Anyone Sick!") but they provide a perfect opportunity to mock the Death Eaters, turning their fearsome tattoo into a harmless treat.

Fever Fudge

ONE OF MANY items offered in the aforementioned Skiving Snackboxes, Fever Fudge is notable for its rather unintended side effects. It was created with the intention that whoever consumed the treat would develop a fever almost immediately: perfect for buying your way out of a day in Potions class. However, the fudge does have a tendency to 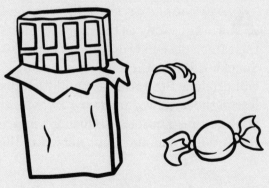 cause the eater to break out in rather nasty boils. It's possible Hogwarts caretaker Argus Filch is a victim of Fever Fudge in the film adaptation of *Harry Potter and the Order of the Phoenix*. After snacking on a box of chocolates, Filch appears in Umbridge's office with a face full of boils.

Shield Hats

SIMILAR TO HEADLESS hats, which have the ability to make it look as though the wearer's head has disappeared completely, Shield Hats are able to protect the person wearing one from a wide range of spells and curses. Although Shield Hats are not particularly helpful against powerful spells such as the Killing Curse, the Ministry still hands them out to wizards during the battle against Voldemort and his acolytes. Their success led to the creation of other shield-themed items from the Weasleys, such as gloves and cloaks.

Nosebleed Nougats

AN EVERGREEN ITEM in the Skiving Snackbox, Nosebleed Nougat works exactly as the name suggests. Snacking on one will cause the eater's nose to erupt in a geyser-like nosebleed. Like all Skiving Snackbox items, the candies are color-coded, so eating the other end will produce the antidote. Quidditch player Katie Bell learns this lesson the hard way in *Harry Potter and the Order of the Phoenix* when, after getting a nosebleed during a match, she eats what she thinks is the antidote end and finds herself in the hospital wing instead.

Dungbombs

ALTHOUGH NOT A Weasley creation, Dungbombs continue to be a popular item at Fred and George's store. As the name implies, Dungbombs are powerful stink bombs that give off an unbelievably putrid odor. They are popular pranks at Hogwarts, and the bane of Argus Filch's existence. By the time of Dolores Umbridge's tyrannical reign at Hogwarts, the students openly rebel against the headmistress by flinging Dungbombs all over the halls. Given that the items are considered a classic in the annals of wizarding pranking, it's no surprise that the Weasleys opt to sell them at their shop.

Trick Wands

ONE OF THE Weasley twins' earliest creations, trick wands look exactly like the real deal, but, when used, either turn into a bizarre object, like a rubber chicken or a haddock, or beat the user about the head. Fred and George worked on the wands for years, as evidenced by their mother's frustration at their leaving them around the Burrow. During the Quidditch World Cup in *Harry Potter and the Goblet of Fire*, Ludo Bagman, the Head of the Department of Magical Games and Sports, is impressed enough with the wands that he offers to buy some—proof to the Weasley twins that they could make a profit off pranks.

JUST DUR-SERTS

AFTER HOW THE DURSLEYS TREAT HARRY AS A CHILD, IT'S HILARIOUSLY SATISFYING WHEN THEY GET THEIRS.

FOLLOWING THE DEATHS of his parents at Voldemort's hands, Harry is forced to live with his only remaining relatives, his mother's sister, Petunia; her husband, Vernon; and their spoiled, obnoxious son, Dudley. The Dursleys are a despicable, awful clan that mistreat Harry every chance they get. So it's no surprise that the best laughs involving the Dursley family tend to come at their expense.

Mail Call at Privet Drive

AT THE OUTSET of *Harry Potter and the Sorcerer's Stone*, Hogwarts continually sends owls to Harry's Privet Drive residence informing him of his acceptance into Hogwarts School of Witchcraft and Wizardry. But the Dursleys continue to intercept the letters, no matter how many of them pile up. Finally, on a Sunday morning, Uncle Vernon seems particularly cheerful because there's no mail on Sundays. He underestimates the persistence of Hogwarts, however, as a hail of letters comes streaming down the fireplace and directly toward his face, forcing the Dursleys to leave the house in a rage.

Dudley Gets a Porcine Makeover

AFTER 11 YEARS of ignorance, Harry gets a crash-course introduction to the magical community in *Harry Potter and the Sorcerer's Stone* when Hagrid barges in on the Dursley family's island hideout to inform the youngster of his birthright. The Dursleys are aghast and immediately challenge Hagrid's authority. The Hogwarts gamekeeper remains relatively placid until Vernon dares to insult Albus Dumbledore. Hagrid, unwilling to tolerate any slander spoken against his headmaster, retaliates by using his magic umbrella to zap a pig's tail onto Dudley's backside. Hagrid notes his intention was to turn Dudley into a pig, but since Dudley already looks so much like one, there wasn't much left to do.

Uncle Vernon Gets a Phone Call

DURING THE SUMMERS, Harry is forced to return back to Privet Drive and live with the Dursleys. Living with his adoptive family is always unpleasant, but their hatred and intolerance of the magical community to which Harry now belongs makes things somehow even worse. A prime example is when Ron decides to give Harry a call a few weeks into the break at the start of *Harry Potter and the Prisoner of Azkaban*. Unfortunately, Ron has never used a telephone (or, as he refers to it later, a "fellytone"), which leads to a frustrating conversation with Uncle Vernon. As Vernon becomes increasingly angry, Ron shouts into the phone, saying, "I — WANT — TO — TALK — TO — HARRY — POTTER!" This glimpse into the disparity between wizard and Muggle technology leaves Vernon angrier than ever.

Harry Scares Dudley With Magic

AFTER RETURNING FROM Hogwarts at the start of *Harry Potter and the Chamber of Secrets*, Harry finally has a leg up on his bullying cousin, Dudley. Unaware Harry is legally forbidden to perform magic until he is 17, Dudley is deathly afraid of what Harry might do to him, perhaps recalling the last time he ended up on the wrong end of a spell courtesy of Hagrid. On Harry's birthday,

Dudley teases him about not getting any birthday cards and calls Hogwarts a "freak place." In retaliation, Harry tells Dudley he has the ability to set the hedges on fire. Dudley steps back as Harry lists off some nonsense incantations— *"Jiggery pokery,"* *"Hocus pocus,"* *"squiggly wiggly"*—sending his cousin streaking back into the house calling for his mother.

Dudley Eats a Magic Treat

THE DURSLEYS' ENCOUNTERS with the magical community invariably end in disaster, and this incident at the start of *Harry Potter and the Goblet of Fire* is a prime example. At the beginning of the book (in a scene sadly excised from the 2005 film adaptation), the Weasleys visit Privet Drive to pick up Harry for the Quidditch World Cup. Before they leave, Fred "accidentally" drops a few candies on the floor. Always in search of a snack, Dudley quickly gobbles one up. Unfortunately for Dudley, the candy turns out to be one of Fred and George's pranks, a little confection called Ton-Tongue Toffee. The candy lives up to its name, swelling Dudley's tongue to the size of a python.

Magical Items

WANDS, REMEMBRALLS, MAGIC EYES:
IF YOU THOUGHT THESE OBJECTS WERE CRAZY
BEFORE, YOU HAVEN'T SEEN ANYTHING YET!
UNLESS YOU HAVE A SNEAKOSCOPE...

Why is it so hard for Muggles to find the Hogwarts Express?
IT COVERS ITS TRACKS.

Did you hear the Hogwarts Express once kept going for two days straight?
IT REALLY NEEDED A BRAKE.

★

Did you hear about the wizard who inherited a magic device that floats in the sky and weaves magic carpets?
YOU MIGHT SAY IT'S A "FAMILY AIR LOOM."

★

Did you hear about the wizard who bought a counterfeit device for spotting his enemies?
IT'S A FAUX-GLASS.

Where is the best place to buy a wizard chess set in Diagon Alley?
AT A PAWN SHOP.

Why was Slytherin's locket such a strong Horcrux?

IT WAS INDE-PENDANT.

Why did Dumbledore clean the Mirror of Erised?
IT WAS REFLECTING BADLY ON HIM.

★

Why did Hagrid's motorcycle fall over?
BECAUSE IT WAS TWO TIRED.

★

How do you look for your shoes at Hogwarts?
WITH A SNEAKER-SCOPE.

★

Why don't the books at Hogwarts fall apart?
THEY'RE SPELLBOUND.

What do squirrels do at Gringotts?
GATHER KNUTS.

I couldn't figure out why the Bludger was getting bigger...
...THEN IT HIT ME.

★

How do Hogwarts Quidditch players get picked for their teams?
WITH THE SPORTING HAT.

★

Why do Death Eaters dip their quills in red ink?
IN CASE THEY NEED TO DRAW BLOOD.

★

Why did Harry sell his Invisibility Cloak?
HE COULDN'T SEE HIMSELF WEARING IT.

What do you call a Time-Turner that doesn't work?
AN HOURGLASS.

Why did Dumbledore have to reboot the Pensieve?

ITS MEMORY WAS ALMOST FULL.

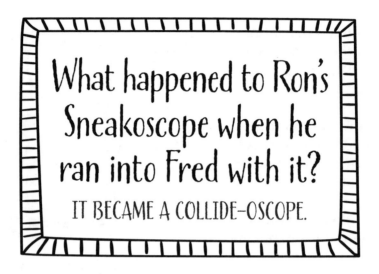

What happened to Ron's Sneakoscope when he ran into Fred with it?

IT BECAME A COLLIDE-OSCOPE.

Why is it so hard to get the conductor on the Hogwarts Express to think of anything else?

HE HAS A ONE-TRACK MIND.

★

Did you hear about the wizard who was overcharged for the Knight Bus?

HE REALLY GOT TAKEN FOR A RIDE.

★

Did you hear the Hogwarts portraits were accused of a crime?

DON'T WORRY, THEY WERE ALL FRAMED.

Why do they play Quidditch on brooms?

WITH THOSE LONG ROBES, VACUUM CLEANERS WOULD BE TOO DANGEROUS.

KNOCK KNOCK.
Who's there?
Remembrall.
Remembrall who?
**Remember-all the
fun times we had at
Hogwarts?**

KNOCK KNOCK.
Who's there?
Wand.
Wand who?
**Wand-a open the
door? It's raining!**

KNOCK KNOCK.
Who's there?
Cauldron.
Cauldron who?
**I called Ron, and he
told me to drop by!**

KNOCK KNOCK.
Who's there?
Quaffle.
Quaffle who?
**It's Quaffle-y cold out!
Open up!**

KNOCK KNOCK.
Who's there?
Knuts.
Knuts who?
**You're Knuts if
you don't let me in!**

KNOCK KNOCK.
Who's there?
Galleon.
Galleon who?
**I drank a Galleon
of pumpkin juice!
Let me in!**

KNOCK KNOCK.
Who's there?
Sickle.
Sickle who?
**I'm Sickle you
locking the door!**

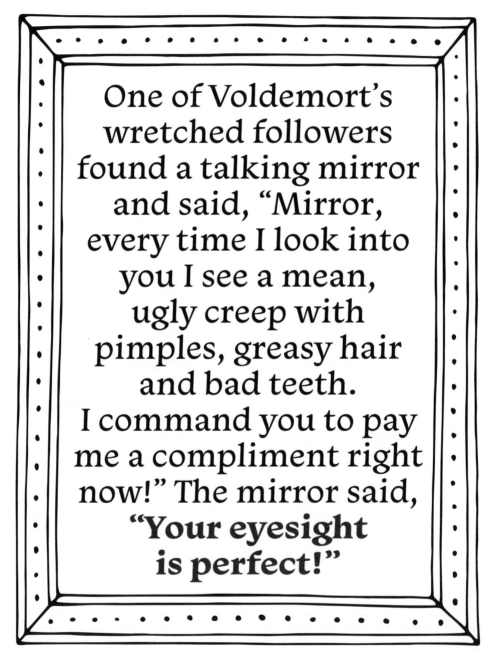

One of Voldemort's wretched followers found a talking mirror and said, "Mirror, every time I look into you I see a mean, ugly creep with pimples, greasy hair and bad teeth. I command you to pay me a compliment right now!" The mirror said, **"Your eyesight is perfect!"**

Does Professor Trelawney know how to use a crystal ball?
SHE SHOULD LOOK INTO IT.

★

Why was Professor Trelawney upset when she broke her crystal ball?
SHE SHOULD HAVE SEEN IT COMING.

★

Why did Harry love his new Nimbus 3000?
IT REALLY SWEPT HIM OFF HIS FEET.

★

What did the wand say when Harry cast *Lumos*?
"NOW IS MY TIME TO SHINE."

Why did the witch disappear from the bathroom?
SHE ACCIDENTALLY FLOO POWDERED HER NOSE.

Why is Mad-Eye Moody like a spare tire?
BOTH ARE KEPT IN A TRUNK.

What do you call a painting of Padfoot?

A PAW-TRAIT.

Why is Professor Trelawney's crystal ball her prized possession?

IT'S WORTH A FORTUNE.

★

Why was Harry self-conscious while wearing his Invisibility Cloak?

HE FELT LIKE EVERYONE COULD SEE RIGHT THROUGH HIM.

★

What happened to the Death Eater when the wizard swung the Sword of Gryffindor at his ankles?

HE WAS DE-FEETED.

What did the Sorting Hat turn into when it gave Harry the Sword of Gryffindor?

THE SWORDING HAT.

How did Dumbledore feel when his Deluminator worked perfectly?

DE-LIGHTED.

★

What do you call a Remembrall that only works occasionally?

A REMEMBER-SOME.

★

Why did Voldemort only see himself in his Foe-Glass?

HE'S ALWAYS BEEN HIS OWN WORST ENEMY.

★

Why does Harry love the Marauder's Map so much?

HE KNOWS HE'D BE LOST WITHOUT IT.

Why can't you find Voldemort on the Marauder's Map?

HIS EVIL IS OFF THE CHARTS.

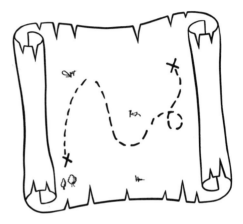

Why were Voldemort's Horcruxes so effective?

HE REALLY PUT HIS SOUL INTO THEM.

Why did Argus Filch volunteer to clean the Mirror of Erised every day?
IT WAS SOMETHING HE COULD SEE HIMSELF DOING.

Did you hear about the time Dumbledore's Deluminator went crazy and took out every light in Hogwarts?
THOSE WERE DARK DAYS.

★

On a scale of 1 to 10, how likely are you to find the Hogwarts Express?
ABOUT 9¾.

★

Did you hear about the wizards who played Exploding Snap in a cheese shop?
THERE WAS DE-BRIE EVERYWHERE.

What happened when Ron put Spellotape on his homework?

HE GOT STUCK ON ONE PARTICULAR PROBLEM.

Have you seen Hagrid's
flying motorcycle?

IT'S WHEELY COOL.

Why did Hagrid
bring his motorcycle
to Madam Pomfrey?

IT NEEDED A FUEL INJECTION.

How did the Death Eater
feel after Hagrid ran him
over on his motorcycle?

TIRED.

Neville had
his Remembrall
confiscated by
Professor Snape.
"Please Professor,"
he said. "I need that
because I'm
so forgetful!"
"And how long have
you had this problem?"
Snape asked.
"What problem?"

Why did Dumbledore give Neville a pair of Omnioculars?

HE FELT HE NEEDED SUPER-VISION.

★

Did you hear that Dumbledore fell off a boat while wearing the Sorting Hat?

HE WAS CAP-SIZED.

★

Why did Draco throw up during Quidditch practice?

HE WAS RIDING A VOMIT 260.

When can you tell Mr. Weasley's Ford is enchanted?

WHENEVER IT TURNS INTO A GAS STATION.

What do you get when you put Floo Powder on a pizza?

A MEAL THAT DELIVERS ITSELF.

How did the wizard fix his blurry Sneakoscope?

HE STARTED A FOCUS GROUP.

Why did Harry steal Voldemort's shoe?
HE WAS TRYING TO DESTROY A PIECE OF HIS SOLE.

★

Did you hear that Voldemort's CD player is a Horcrux?
IT ONLY PLAYS SOUL MUSIC.

★

Harry came to Professor Dumbledore's office wearing his Invisibility Cloak.
DUMBLEDORE SAID, "HARRY, I CAN'T SEE YOU RIGHT NOW."

★

I thought about making the Sword of Gryffindor invisible.
BUT I COULDN'T SEE THE POINT.

What do Chocolate Frogs do when the Knight Bus arrives?
HOP ON.

A wizard walked into a shop in Diagon Alley.

"Hello," he said to the shopkeeper. "Do you sell Remembralls? My memory is so bad I've lost my job."

"That's terrible," the shopkeeper said. "We're hiring if you need a job..."

"No, I'm still employed," the wizard said. "I just can't remember where!"

**What does the
Sorting Hat like to drink
in the morning?**

A CAP-PUCCINO.

★

**What does Mad-Eye Moody
use to wash his eye?**

MOIST-YOUR-EYES-SIR.

★

**How much does a
Deluminator weigh?**

IT'S PRETTY LIGHT.

★

**I got a Howler in
the mail this morning.**

IT WAS A REAL SCREAM.

**Hermione's handbag was
very helpful when escaping
from the Snatchers.**

IT WAS BOTH A
BLESSING AND A PURSE.

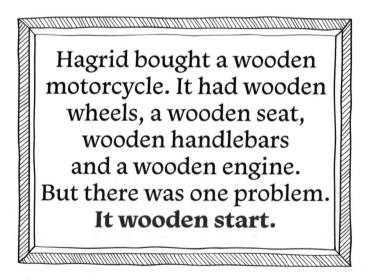

Hagrid bought a wooden
motorcycle. It had wooden
wheels, a wooden seat,
wooden handlebars
and a wooden engine.
But there was one problem.
It wooden start.

Why was Harry's broom late
for Quidditch practice?

IT OVER-SWEPT.

How warm do they keep
the Hogwarts Quidditch pitch?

USUALLY IT'S AT BROOM TEMPERATURE.

Did you hear Harry was
attacked by a hexed Nimbus 3000?

IT WAS A REAL BRUSH WITH DEATH.

I heard the Gryffindor
Quidditch team got new brooms.

THEY SWEPT ALL THE OTHER
HOUSES IN THE PLAYOFFS.

**Why is it hard to trust
the Sorting Hat?**
IT'S ALWAYS TRYING TO
COVER SOMETHING UP.

★

**I got the Omnioculars
I was hoping for.**
THINGS ARE FINALLY LOOKING UP.

★

**Do dragons like
Exploding Snap?**
NO, BUT A DINO MIGHT...

★

**Why did Draco back down
from Ron when he saw he had
Dumbledore's Deluminator?**
HE WAS AFRAID RON WOULD
PUT HIS LIGHTS OUT.

**Why did Professor
Lockhart start
playing Gobstones?**
HE'D LOST HIS MARBLES.

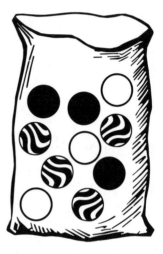

Did you hear
the joke about
the Howler?
NO ONE LIKED THE DELIVERY.

What do you say during a particularly boring game of wizard chess?

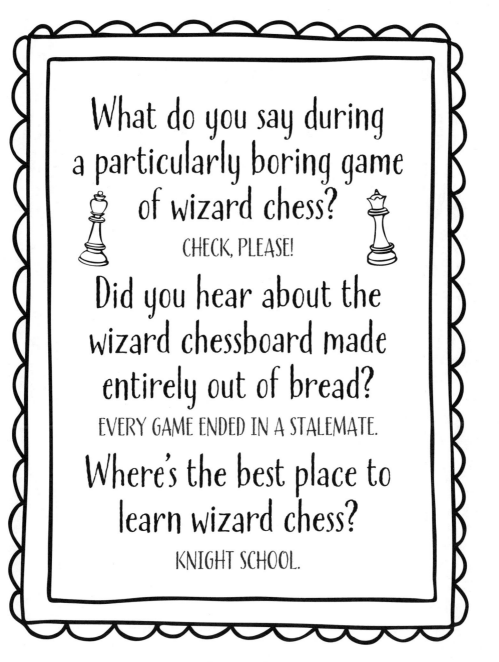

CHECK, PLEASE!

Did you hear about the wizard chessboard made entirely out of bread?

EVERY GAME ENDED IN A STALEMATE.

Where's the best place to learn wizard chess?

KNIGHT SCHOOL.

IS PEEVES THE POLTERGEIST THE FUNNIEST CHARACTER IN THE BOOKS?

A SOURCE OF HIGH COMEDY IN THE NOVELS, PEEVES WAS EXORCISED FROM THE MOVIES ENTIRELY. BUT THIS PESKY POLTERGEIST DESERVES A PLACE IN THE PANTHEON OF COMEDY.

HOGWARTS IS FILLED with ghosts of various kinds, from the Bloody Baron to Nearly Headless Nick. But one of the most infamous from the books, Peeves the Poltergeist, never made the leap to the big screen. A resident of Hogwarts since its founding more than 1,000 years before Harry arrives, Peeves is known for making all sorts of mischief and making the lives of both students and professors difficult. A major fixture in the novels, Peeves had been slated to make his big-screen debut in 2001's *Harry Potter and the Sorcerer's Stone*, with the late British comic Rik Mayall cast in the role. However, his scenes were cut from the film and have yet to see the light of day. In case you want to know why Peeves is such a classic comedic character, here are just a few examples.

He's an Equal-Opportunity Offender

UNLIKE MANY IN the *Harry Potter* universe, Peeves never chooses sides: He torments just about everyone equally. Although he definitely enjoys making life difficult for Hogwarts students, Peeves's sense of equality when it comes to teasing can also work to their advantage. In *Harry Potter and the Sorcerer's Stone*, Harry, Ron and Hermione are skulking about the castle after hours when Peeves spots them and summons Argus Filch. However, when the caretaker shows up, Peeves decides to have a little fun, asking Filch to say "please" and telling him, "Shan't say nothing if you don't say please." When Filch relents, Peeves gleefully says, "Nothing!" before floating off down the hall.

He's Good With a Song

PEEVES IS VERY creative in his mockery and antics, often devising songs to further antagonize his victims. In *Harry Potter and the Chamber of Secrets*, Peeves takes great pleasure in the school rumor that Harry is the one responsible for unleashing the mysterious beast from the Chamber of Secrets, crafting a song he sings while floating behind Harry: "Oh, Potter, you rotter, oh, what have you done/ You're killing off students, you think it's good fun!"

He Can Appreciate His Peers

ALTHOUGH PEEVES DOESN'T treat any of the students at Hogwarts with anything close to respect, he also acknowledges a kindred spirit when he feels it's warranted. After Fred and George create a ruckus departing Hogwarts in *Harry Potter and the Order of the Phoenix*, they stop and tell Peeves to keep making Dolores Umbridge's life miserable. Peeves, who has never done anything a Hogwarts student asks him to, removes his cap and gives Fred and George a salute as they speed off into the sunset. She's in good hands.

He Can Work With a Partner

SOME OF THE best comedy acts in history weren't singular stand-ups—they were duos or groups. Peeves is very much a solo act, preferring to irritate Hogwarts students and staff without input or interference from others, but he isn't above teaming up when the occasion calls for it. During the reign of Dolores Umbridge in *Harry Potter and the Order of the Phoenix*, Peeves unscrews a chandelier in an effort to upset Umbridge's constant crusade for order. As Harry notices Professor McGonagall walking past Peeves, he is certain he hears the professor whisper, "It unscrews the other way."

He Knows His Audience

FOR PEEVES, HOGWARTS is the ultimate playground. He can throw water balloons at students who've come in from the rain, write rude words on chalkboards or change Christmas songs to vulgar ditties, all without fear of repercussions. But he never dares put an incorporeal toe out of line around Albus Dumbledore. In fact, he's overly respectful around the Hogwarts headmaster, even adopting a different manner of speech to sound more deferential. Like any good comedian, Peeves is smart enough to know he's found the venue of a lifetime. It's a gig he intends to keep.

Castles and Locales

WANT TO FIND THE FUNNY IN THE MAGICAL WORLD?
PULL OUT YOUR MARAUDER'S MAP AND SEEK OUT
SOME SILLINESS AT THESE LAUGH-TASTIC LOCALES!

What did the seventh-year say to the first-year who didn't understand how to get to Platform 9¾?
"LET ME RUN THROUGH IT AGAIN..."

★

What did the termite say when he walked into the Hog's Head?
"IS THE BAR TENDER HERE?"

★

I heard Voldemort went to a tavern in Diagon Alley called the Fiddle Tavern.
NOW IT'S THE VILE INN.

Why are giants' taverns more popular than other taverns?
THEY SET A VERY HIGH BAR.

Why are there so many environmentalists in the Slytherin common room?

BECAUSE IT'S THE GREEN HOUSE.

What is one word in the magical
community that contains
a whole sentence?

AZKABAN.

What would you call Fawkes
if he went to Azkaban?

A JAILBIRD.

Why can't wizards make
phone calls at Azkaban?

THE CELL SERVICE IS TERRIBLE.

Who provides the
entertainment
in wizard prison?

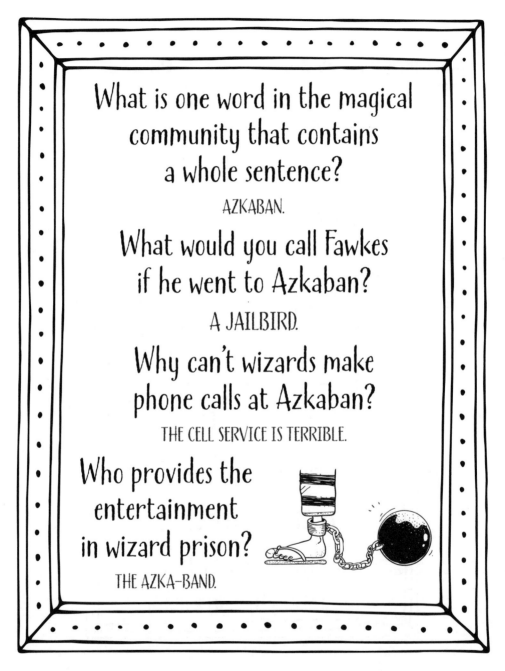

THE AZKA–BAND.

Why did the Malfoys' butler quit?
HE REFUSED TO BE ORDERED AROUND IN THAT MANOR.

What's hollow but filled with people?
GODRIC'S HOLLOW.

★

I heard a bunch of black birds took over the Hog's Head.
NOW IT'S A CROW BAR.

★

I heard about the wizard who wanted to live in a talking house.
YES, IN A MANOR OF SPEAKING.

★

Where do ghosts study in the magical world?
BOO-BATONS.

I heard there is a tavern at the bottom of the Great Lake.

IT'S A REAL DIVE.

What kind of money do deer keep at Gringotts?

DOE KNUTS.

What does Fawkes keep at Gringotts?

A NEST EGG.

What did the goblin say when Bellatrix Lestrange realized she'd been robbed at Gringotts?

"IT'S NOT MY VAULT!"

What is the motto of Gringotts?

LOANS SWEET LOANS.

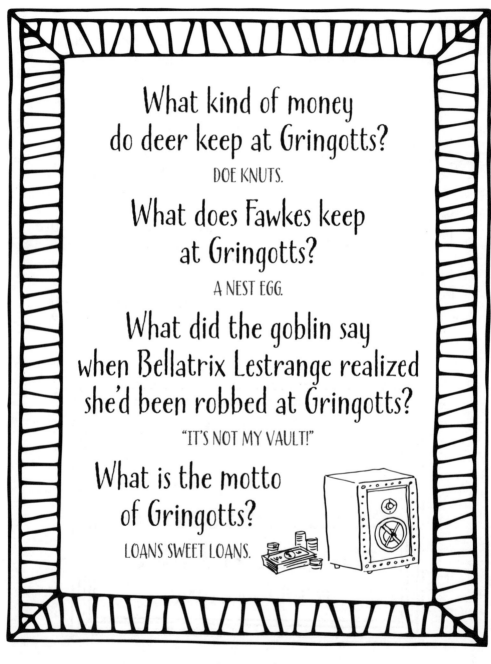

Why did the wizard lose all his houses?

HE DIDN'T KNOW HOW TO MIND HIS MANORS.

★

What do you call a pair of Quidditch players who live in the same dormitory?

BROOM-MATES.

★

Did you hear they're doing renovations at 12 Grimmauld Place?

THEY'RE LOOKING TO EXPAND.

I just bought a 100-year-old wig at Borgin and Burkes.

IT'S A REAL HAIR-LOOM!

How do Harry, Ron and Hermione get into their House common room?

THROUGH THE GRYFFIN-DOOR.

A weasel walks
into the Leaky Cauldron.
"What can I get you?"
asks the bartender.
"Pop!" goes the weasel.

A skeleton walks
into the Leaky Cauldron.
"Gimme a butterbeer,"
he says. **"And a mop!"**

A Pumpkin Pasty walks
into the Leaky Cauldron.
The bartender shakes
his head and says,
**"Sorry, pal. We don't
serve food here."**

I heard there was a problem with the plumbing at Hogwarts.

NOW IT'S CALLED CLOGWARTS.

Where's the best place to find blueprints in the magical world?
DIAGRAM ALLEY.

★

How do you know the Whomping Willow is leaving Hogwarts?
ITS TRUNK IS PACKED.

★

How many wizards can jump higher than the Shrieking Shack?
ALL OF THEM. THE SHRIEKING SHACK CAN'T JUMP!

Why did Harry use the bathtub in the Prefects' Bathroom to unlock the Triwizard egg?
HE WAS HOPING HE COULD FAUCET OPEN.

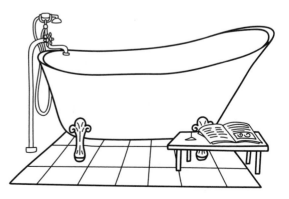

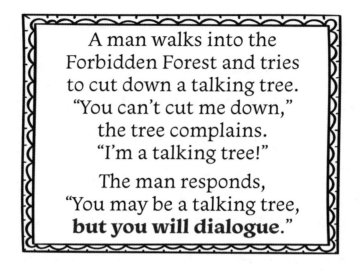

A man walks into the Forbidden Forest and tries to cut down a talking tree.
"You can't cut me down," the tree complains. "I'm a talking tree!"

The man responds, "You may be a talking tree, **but you will dialogue**."

I heard the plans to build a bouncy house replica of Hogwarts were scrapped.

BLAME IT ON INFLATION.

What do the owls in the Owlery do together?

A LOT OF MAIL BONDING.

★

I bought a box of talking light bulbs in Diagon Alley.

THEY SEEMED BRIGHT.

★

Did you hear Dumbledore built a device to raise and lower the Hogwarts drawbridge automatically?

IT'S A RE-MOAT CONTROL.

★

What do they serve for breakfast at Azkaban?

BAGELS AND LOX.

Why did Harry love to visit the flower shop in Diagon Alley so much?
BECAUSE HE'S A POTTER!

Why did Harry look for Horcruxes in the House of Blues?
IT'S WHERE THEY HAVE THE MOST SOUL.

★

What is Knockturn Alley's vaccine clinic called?
A SHOT IN THE DARK.

★

All the clothes at Madam Malkin's were having a competition to see which was the coolest.
IT ENDED UP BEING A TIE.

Where do death eaters go after they testify against Voldemort?
INTO THE WITCHES PROTECTION PROGRAM.

Where do evil wizards do their shopping?

VOLDE MART.

Did you hear about the clock with no hands at Hogwarts?

IT'S A TIMELESS TREASURE.

I heard they sell rubber money in Diagon Alley.

FOR PEOPLE WHO WANT TO STRETCH THEIR BUDGET.

★

Why should you be quiet in Snape's classroom?

YOU MIGHT WAKE THE SLEEPING POTIONS.

★

Why can't you ever get an appointment at Flourish and Blotts?

THEY'RE FULLY BOOKED.

A duck walks into the Apothecary in Diagon Alley to buy some chapstick.
"JUST PUT IT ON MY BILL," HE SAYS.

What's the tallest building in Diagon Alley?
FLOURISH AND BLOTTS.
IT HAS THE MOST STORIES!

★

Why can't you trust the stairs at Hogwarts?
THEY'RE ALWAYS UP TO SOMETHING.

★

Do they take class trips at Hogwarts?
ONLY WHEN PEEVES LEAVES
BROOMSTICKS LYING ROUND!

★

What happened to Voldemort during the Battle of Hogwarts?
HE HAD A BAD HEIR DAY.

A wizard walks into Madam Malkin's and says, "I want to try on the robes in the front window." "Sir," said the owner. **"You'll have to use the dressing room like everyone else."**

What happened when they opened a Gringotts branch at the North Pole?

ALL THE ASSETS WERE FROZEN.

Did you hear that a Dark wizard robbed Sugarplum's Sweet Shop?

HE REALLY TAKES THE CAKE!

★

Did you hear about the 10-million-Galleon toilet stolen from the Ministry of Magic?

THE AURORS HAVE NOTHING TO GO ON.

★

What's it like working at the Azkaban library?

IT HAS PROSE AND CONS.

Someone stole a broken scale from Borgin and Burkes.

HE WON'T GET A WEIGH WITH IT.

A wizard walks into the
Leaky Cauldron and sits at the bar.

"Those robes look great on you!"
a voice says suddenly.
The wizard looks around,
but doesn't see anyone.

"And that beard is very handsome!"
says another voice.
The wizard looks around again
but still can't figure out where
the voices are coming from.

"Have you been working out?"
says another voice.

Now the wizard is really startled.
He stands up and calls for
the bartender. "Where are these
voices coming from?" he asks.

**"Oh, those are the peanuts,"
says the bartender.
"They're complimentary."**

KNOCK KNOCK.
Who's there?
Diagon.
Diagon who?
**Duh, i-a-gone and
locked myself out!**

KNOCK KNOCK.
Who's there?
Azkaban.
Azkaban who?
**Azka-banned from
the house, but let
me in anyway!**

KNOCK KNOCK.
Who's there?
Privet.
Privet who?
**I can't tell you,
it's Privet!**

KNOCK KNOCK.
Who's there?
Hogsmeade.
Hogsmeade who?
**Hogsmeade a
mess and I need
to come in!**

KNOCK KNOCK.
Who's there?
Manor.
Manor who?
**Can the manor the
house let me in?**

KNOCK KNOCK.
Who's there?
Gringotts.
Gringotts who?
**Gring-gots to be
kidding me that the
door is locked!**

KNOCK KNOCK.
Who's there?
Hollow.
Hollow who?
Hollow! I think you know who it is!

KNOCK KNOCK.
Who's there?
Wizarding school.
Wizarding school who?
Wizarding's cool, but I'm ready to come in now.

KNOCK KNOCK.
Who's there?
Knockturn.
Knockturn who?
Do Knockturn around without opening this door!

What do they serve butterbeer in at the Three Broomsticks?
BUTTERCUPS.

★

Why do Harry and Ron shop so well together?
THEY'RE DIAGON ALLIES.

★

Did you hear about the clairvoyant elf who escaped Azkaban?
THERE'S A SMALL MEDIUM AT LARGE.

★

Where do German Dark wizards go?
KNOCKWURST ALLEY!

★

What do Azkaban prisoners say when they bump into the warden?
PARDON ME, SIR!

★

What class do Death Eaters enjoy the most?
DARK ARTS & CRAFTS.

What do you wear to
a pool party in the
Forbidden Forest?

SWIMMING TRUNKS.

What's the best way to access the
internet in the Forbidden Forest?

LOG ON.

What kinds of movies are most
popular in the Forbidden Forest?

SAPPY MOVIES.

How did the wizard get
lost trying to find his way out
of the Forbidden Forest?

HE GOT STUMPED.

A wizard walks into the Leaky Cauldron with a Niffler on his shoulder.

"That's neat!" says the bartender. "Where did you find it?"

"Hogwarts," says the Niffler. "They've got loads of them there!"

Have you seen all the artwork on display in Hogwarts?

IT'S VERY AD-MURAL-BLE!

I heard the Whomping Willow might be moving to a new school.

IT'S REALLY BRANCHING OUT.

★

Who usually shops at Ollivanders?

WAND-ERING SOULS.

★

What happens if you take the Hogwarts Express home?

YOU STILL HAVE TO BRING IT BACK.

**Did you hear there
was a bad case of measles
at Azkaban?**

NEARLY EVERYBODY BROKE OUT.

★

**I heard Hogwarts has
a new science teacher.**

HIS NAME IS PROFESSOR AL CHEMY.

★

**I heard there's a
problem with the
staircases at Hogwarts.**

THE SITUATION SEEMS
TO BE ESCALATING.

What do you say to
get the Whomping
Willow to stop?

LEAF ME ALONE!

The harbormaster
at Beauxbatons
was showing
Madame Maxime
all of the school's ships.

"Here is un, deux, trois,
quatre, six, sept..."

"Wait," said
Madame Maxime.

"Where is the fifth ship?"

"Cinq*."

*French for "five," and pronounced "sank"

THE FUNNIEST CREATURES IN *HARRY POTTER*

THE WIZARDING WORLD IS FILLED WITH ALL SORTS OF BIZARRE ANIMALS, SOME CUTE AND CUDDLY, OTHERS FEARSOME AND FRIGHTENING—BUT ALL EASY TO LAUGH ABOUT UNDER THE RIGHT CIRCUMSTANCES.

FOR MUGGLES, THE animal world is pretty straightforward. There are some, like dogs and cats, that make great pets, and others, like tigers and sharks (or tiger sharks), that do not. But the magical world is a little different. Some animals that you would never imagine bringing home make great companions and others that seem harmless and adorable would devour you without batting an eyelash. So how do you tell who's a pet and who's a threat? Start with the ones that at least provide a few laughs.

Errol

THE WEASLEY FAMILY'S elderly, long-suffering owl, Errol is most likely too old, and possibly too senile, to be delivering messages to Ron and his siblings at Hogwarts. But due to the Weasley's limited financial means, Errol is stuck with the job. The owl is forever shedding feathers and his bad eyesight means that he is always crashing into things, from windows to tableware in the Great Hall. His perpetual pratfalls, coupled with Ron's, "Bloody bird," make for some lighthearted moments in the early days of the series.

Boggarts

THESE POLTERGEIST-LIKE creatures are not inherently funny, as they take the form of whatever scares the person who encounters them the most. However, if that person knows the spell to defeat a boggart, that's when the laughs come in. By uttering the incantation, *Riddikulus*, the wizard will turn the boggart into something much more comical and humorous. For example, the

giant spider meant to frighten Ron is incapacitated with eight pairs of magically summoned roller skates, making the arachnid terror a harmless klutz.

Dobby

HARRY'S FIRST ENCOUNTER with a house-elf, the unseen servants of the magical world, is certainly a memorable one. Dobby first appears in *Harry Potter and the Chamber of Secrets*, showing up in Harry's Muggle home to try to keep him from returning to Hogwarts. In an effort to prevent Harry from leaving Privet Drive, Dobby drops an entire cake on the wife of Uncle Vernon's boss. He seals the entrance to Platform 9¾ and later sends a rogue Bludger after Harry to try and take him out of commission. In the moment, these close encounters aren't particularly funny. But once Harry is safely past Dobby's antics, the lack of subtlety with which Dobby goes about his attempted sabotage can make even the Boy Who Lived chuckle. Beneath Dobby's hapless exterior, though, lies the heart of a hero, as he eventually proves by the series's end.

Mandrakes

MAGICAL PLANTS THAT vaguely resemble humans, mandrakes are best known for the loud, piercing scream they unleash when uprooted from the ground. The scream of a young mandrake is powerful enough to knock out a person within earshot, while an older mandrake's cries can be lethal to anyone not wearing ear protection, which is why Hogwarts students don earmuffs before interacting with these creatures. Mandrakes also have a playful and raucous nature, as evidenced by the loud party they throw in the greenhouse once they reach adolescence in *Harry Potter and the Chamber of Secrets*.

Cornish Pixies

THESE IMPISH CREATURES are born to create havoc, and they get their chance thanks to Professor Lockhart in *Harry Potter and the Chamber of Secrets*. Lockhart figures the creatures would be perfect for relaying a lesson on self-defense. However, he is completely unprepared for the chaos they create when turned loose. The tiny blue sprites go berserk in the classroom, tearing things apart and even going after some of the students. Thanks to a freezing charm from Hermione, the pixies' rampage is finally cut short.

Nifflers

TINY CREATURES THAT look like a cross between a mole and a platypus, Nifflers are highly coveted in the magical world for their love of shiny things, which makes them great treasure hunters. Their bellies contain pouches that can hold an almost unfathomable amount of gold, silver and other sparkly trinkets. A Niffler accompanies Newt Scamander on his 1926 journey to New York City, where the creature's fixation on shiny objects leads to an attempted robbery of a jewelry store and bank.

The Monster Book of Monsters

THE OLD SAYING warns to not judge a book by its cover, and in this case, that is sage advice. *The Monster Book of Monsters* isn't just a book, it's also a monster itself—one with the tendency to bite the extremities of careless readers. Ron himself becomes a victim of the book's toothy proclivities, receiving a bite on the ankle on one occasion. The only way to soothe this literary beast is to stroke its spine. That is, if you can even summon the courage to pick it up.

Blast-Ended Skrewts

A GRUESOME CROSS BETWEEN a fire crab and a manticore bred by Hagrid in a massive victory for "coulda" over "shoulda," these creatures move themselves along by blasting fire out of their rear ends and are known for their ill tempers. Hagrid attempts to bring them into his Care of Magical Creatures class for a little education, but this proves to be a poor idea. Ornery armored beasts that fart fireballs: What could have possibly gone wrong?

Fluffy

O NLY RUBEUS HAGRID would decide to give a vicious, gigantic three-headed dog a name like Fluffy. The oversized beast is charged with guarding the Sorcerer's Stone, his fearsome appearance enough of a deterrent to ensure the Stone would not be disturbed by anyone. However, it turned out that Fluffy had a softer side, as he can be lulled  to sleep by the gentle strains of music. Thanks to a flute Hagrid gave Harry for Christmas, Harry, Ron and Hermione are able to soothe the savage beast and reach the Stone without issue.

Dark Magic

THESE JOKES ARE SO HILARIOUS, THEY'RE UNFORGIVABLE. YOU'LL BE LAUGHING SO HARD, YOUR RIBS WILL FEEL LIKE YOU'VE BEEN HIT WITH THE CRUCIATUS CURSE!

What does a forgetful wizard call Voldemort?

HE-WHO-CAN-NOT-BE-REMEMBERED.

Who handles Voldemort's money?

HIS OCCULTANT.

★

Who do Dark wizards date?

THEIR GHOUL-FRIENDS.

★

What is a Death Eater's favorite takeout dish?

AVADA KEBAB-RA.

★

What is Narcissa Malfoy to Lucius?

HIS HEX-WIFE.

★

Is Peter Pettigrew skilled at curses?

HE HAS AVADA KE-DABBLED.

What do you call a lousy riddle? VOLDEMORT.

Why do the female Death Eaters love Voldemort?

HE HAS HEX APPEAL.

I heard they're making a series of interconnected movies about Voldemort.

IT'S CALLED THE MARVOLO CINEMATIC UNIVERSE.

★

How did Harry end up in the cemetery with Voldemort?

HE MADE A GRAVE MISTAKE.

★

Why did the witch dump her demon boyfriend?

HE WAS TOO POSSESSIVE.

★

How do Death Eaters buy gas?

BY THE GALLEON.

Where can witches learn about Dark magic when they're not at Hogwarts?

WICCA-PEDIA.

How can you contact spirits and clean your windows at the same time?
WITH A SQUEEGEE BOARD.

Why was the duck sent to Azkaban?
FOR PRACTICING FOWL MAGIC.

★

Where can you learn how to contact spirits at Hogwarts?
SEANCE CLASS.

★

Why didn't the book of Dark magic work?
THE AUTHOR FORGOT TO DO A SPELL CHECK.

★

What do you call a bunch of Inferi in a row?
A DEADLINE.

What happens if you don't pay your exorcist?
YOU GET RE-POSSESSED.

KNOCK KNOCK.
Who's there?
Voodoo.
Voodoo who?
**Voodoo you
think you are?**

KNOCK KNOCK.
Who's there?
Babbling curse.
Babbling curse who?
**Babbling curse
I'm so angry you
locked me out!**

KNOCK KNOCK.
Who's there?
Gaunt.
Gaunt who?
**Gaunt to get inside,
it's cold out here!**

KNOCK KNOCK.
Who's there?
Dementor.
Dementor who?
**Dementor bring my
key when I left,
but I forgot!**

KNOCK KNOCK.
Who's there?
**He-Who-Must-
Not-Be-Named.**
He-Who-Must-
Not-Be-Named who?
**I just told you I must
not be named!**

KNOCK KNOCK.
Who's there?
Draco.
Draco who?
**I Draco too much:
I need to go to the
bathroom!**

KNOCK KNOCK.
Who's there?
Charm.
Charm who?
**Charm is tired from
knocking so much!**

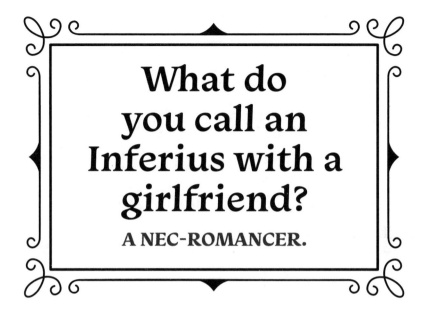

What do you call an Inferius with a girlfriend?

A NEC-ROMANCER.

Why does Voldemort hate the beach?

HIS SUNGLASSES WON'T STAY ON.

Where do Dark wizards go when they can't get into Hogwarts?

CHARM SCHOOL.

★

Where do Dark wizards buy their clothes?

ABERZOMBIE & WITCH.

★

Why is it hard to trust Professor Quirrell?

HE'S TWO-FACED.

★

How do ghost bullies communicate?

WITH A WEDGIE BOARD.

Fred once called George in a panic and shouted, "An evil wizard turned me into a tiny harp! I don't know what to do!" Frantically, George scrambled to his brother only to find out...

...he's really a big lyre.

A wizard went to a Tarot card reader in Knockturn Alley. "How's business?" he asked her.

"UNPREDICTABLE."

★

What kind of makeup does Bellatrix Lestrange wear?

MA-SCARE-A.

★

What does Professor Quirrell use to look up words?

TURBAN DICTIONARY.

★

What's a Death Eater's favorite shape?

A HEX-AGON.

Why did the Death Eater stop working on his voodoo doll?

HE DECIDED TO PUT A PIN IN IT FOR NOW.

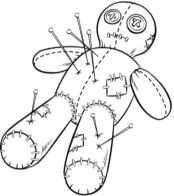

What does Voldemort use for -+- sunburn? -+-

THE DEATHLY ALOES.

How does Voldemort write down his evil plans?

WITH A DARK MARK-ER.

Why is Lucius Malfoy afraid of his broom?

IT'S BEEN GATHERING DIRT ON HIM FOR YEARS.

I heard Voldemort made a voodoo doll of me.

I THINK HE'S PULLING MY LEG.

★

What did Nagini say after Voldemort let her attack Snape?

"FANGS A LOT!"

★

Why did the witch break up with the necromancer?

HE JUST WANTED HER FOR HER BODY.

★

Why didn't Snape show up at James and Lily Potter's wedding?

HE NEVER RECEIVED AN INCANTATION.

A Slytherin called to a Gryffindor across the Great Hall. "Hey," she said. "Do you have stabbing pain like someone is sticking pins in a voodoo doll of you? "No," came the reply. **"How about now?"**

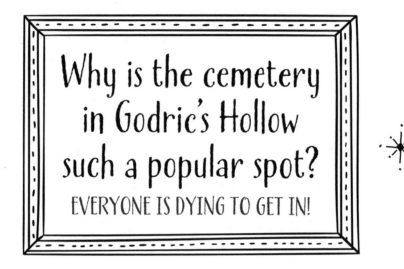

Why is the cemetery in Godric's Hollow such a popular spot?
EVERYONE IS DYING TO GET IN!

How do you know if Voldemort used the bathroom before you?

HE LEAVES A DARK MARK.

★

How could Voldemort have defeated Harry?

HE COULD HAVE HIDDEN THE LAST HORCRUX IN HIS NOSE.

★

How do you know Voldemort cares about Harry's education?

HE ALWAYS WAITS UNTIL THE END OF THE SCHOOL YEAR TO TRY TO KILL HIM.

What's the best way to keep evil spirits out of your house?

EXORCISE REGULARLY.

Why did Peter Pettigrew steal desserts from the Great Hall?
BECAUSE HE WAS A PIE-RAT!

How does Voldemort look for his No. 1 enemy?
WITH HARRY SPOTTERS.

★

What is the one thing the Dark Lord can never do?
USE A TISSUE.

★

What did Voldemort do when Harry escaped?
THREW A HISS-Y FIT.

★

Nagini walks into the Three Broomsticks.
THE BARTENDER ASKS "HOW DID YOU DO THAT?"

Why are there no portraits of Voldemort anywhere?

BECAUSE HE'S HE-WHO-MUST-NOT-BE-FRAMED.

Why couldn't Voldemort get any of the Hogwarts spirits to answer his texts?
THEY ALL GHOSTED HIM.

Why are Death Eaters like luggage?
THEY TRAVEL IN PACKS.

★

What is a Death Eater's blood type?
PURE.

★

What does a wizard say to hypnotize his broom?
"YOU ARE GETTING VERY SWEEPY..."

★

Why did one necromancer marry the other?
THEY WANTED TO RAISE A FAMILY TOGETHER.

Why did the Death Eater cross the road?

BECAUSE VOLDEMORT TOLD HIM TO.

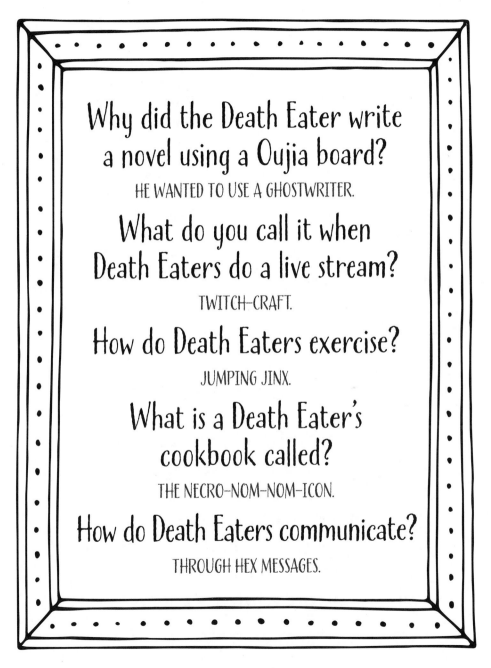

Why did the Death Eater write a novel using a Oujia board?

HE WANTED TO USE A GHOSTWRITER.

What do you call it when Death Eaters do a live stream?

TWITCH-CRAFT.

How do Death Eaters exercise?

JUMPING JINX.

What is a Death Eater's cookbook called?

THE NECRO-NOM-NOM-ICON.

How do Death Eaters communicate?

THROUGH HEX MESSAGES.

**Did you hear about
the Death Eater who
couldn't spell?**

HE SOLD HIS SOUL TO SANTA.

**Why was Salazar
Slytherin so popular
with his classmates?**

THEY THOUGHT HE WAS HISS-TERICAL.

★

**I heard they're selling
a cursed wig in
Knockturn Alley.**

IT'S A HELL TOUPEE.

★

**Have you heard that
there have been cutbacks in
Voldemort's organization?**

MOST OF THE DEATH EATERS
HAVE BEEN OUT-SORCE'D.

A Death Eater was trying
to contact a dark spirit.
Unfortunately, he read the
incantation wrong, then
tripped over the candles.
**I guess two wrongs
don't make a rite.**

How would Voldemort
pick his nose?

FROM A CATALOG.

Why can you trust Voldemort
with your secrets?

HE'S NOT NOSY.

How does Voldemort
smell without a nose?

TERRIBLY!

How did Voldemort
lose his nose?

IT WOULDN'T STOP RUNNING.

How many wizards does it take to change a lightbulb?

Six.

One Slytherin to break it.

One Gryffindor to volunteer to change it.

Three Hufflepuffs to hold the ladder to ensure the safety of the Gryffindor student.

And one Ravenclaw to point out that **they could have just used magic in the first place.**

During Voldemort's reign, a wizard was cursed every 30 seconds.

THAT POOR GUY!

★

What did young Delphini use to make brownies?

AN EASY-BAKE COVEN.

★

What does an Inferius blow his nose with?

BRAIN TISSUE.

★

Voldemort is so evil...

HE EVEN CUT OFF HIS NOSE TO SPITE HIS FACE.

In addition to the Horcrux, what is Voldemort's other favorite ring?

SUFFER-RING.

Why didn't Voldemort buy a device to view his memories?

IT WAS TOO EX-PENSIEVE.

THE SPELLS THAT WENT COMICALLY WRONG

MAGIC IN THE WIZARDING WORLD IS NO LAUGHING MATTER, EXCEPT IN THESE CASES.

BEING A WIZARD doesn't mean you're automatically going to be a master (or mistress) of magic. Why do you think there's a school for this sort of thing? But even those who have graduated from Hogwarts (or Durmstrang, or Beauxbatons) still find that magic can sometimes backfire. Here are just a few examples of newbie wizards and seasoned mages who let their wands get away from them.

Harry Has a Bone to Pick with Lockhart

AFTER BREAKING HIS arm during a Quidditch match in *Harry Potter and the Chamber of Secrets* thanks to a rogue Bludger that was aiming for his head, Harry finds himself at the mercy of Gilderoy Lockhart, who assures everyone present that he can mend Harry's arm with a simple spell. Sadly for Harry, he gets his first indication that Lockhart may not be the wizard he claims to be: Instead of healing his broken bones, Lockhart removes all of the bones from his arm, leaving behind a flabby, empty limb.

Ron Ends Up Bewitched

IN HARRY POTTER *and the Half-Blood Prince*, Romilda Vane's crush on Harry drives her to procure some chocolates that are infused with a love potion. But love has a way of complicating things and, when Ron accidentally ingests the chocolates, he falls for Romilda instead. This leads to a brawl between Harry and Ron when Ron, still under the potion's effects, believes Harry wasn't taking his unrequited crush on Romilda seriously.

Harry Becomes an Unwitting Snake Charmer

IN *HARRY POTTER and the Sorcerer's Stone*, before Harry makes the discovery that he comes from a long line of wizards, he and the Durlseys visit the zoo for Dudley's birthday. While looking at a boa constrictor in the reptile house, Harry suddenly discovers he can communicate with reptiles, striking up a conversation with the constrictor. As Harry and the snake are talking, the glass suddenly disappears, setting the snake free and terrifying Dudley and his friends. Maybe this is one backfired spell that actually went right.

Ron Gets Slugged

IN *HARRY POTTER and the Chamber of Secrets*, Ron finds himself cursed with a secondhand wand that then gets snapped during his unplanned flight with Harry in Arthur Weasley's Ford Anglia and subsequent crash into the Whomping Willow. Although the wand is repaired with Spellotape, it still doesn't quite work as intended, a lesson Ron learns when he tries to curse Draco, only to have the spell blow up in his face, causing him to begin vomiting slugs incessantly.

Harry (Sort of) Blows Up His Aunt

AT THE BEGINNING of *Harry Potter and the Prisoner of Azkaban*, Harry is forced to endure a visit from Vernon's sister, Marge. Boorish, loud and often drunk, Marge takes great pleasure in berating Harry every chance she gets. Harry tends to let most of her insults slide, but when Marge goes after his parents and insults their memory, Harry has had enough. He loses his temper and, with it, control of his magic, inadvertently causing Marge to inflate like a balloon and slowly rise up and out of the house. Eventually, the Ministry of Magic has her deflated and her memory erased, but she no doubt, even subconsciously, thought twice before disparaging the Potter clan again.

Hermione Experiences a Cat-astrophe

IN *HARRY POTTER* and the *Chamber of Secrets*, Ron, Harry and Hermione attempt a bit of subterfuge to uncover the truth behind the titular chamber. Using Polyjuice Potion, they plan to disguise themselves as Slytherins in the hopes that someone inside that House might have some answers. However, Hermione makes a crucial error when, while of plucking a hair from  a Slytherin girl's robe for the potion, she grabs some errant cat hair. The result is a ghastly cross between Hermione and a cat that's more terrifying than any basilisk could ever hope to be.

Seamus Finnigan Bungles Booze

DURING HIS FIRST year at Hogwarts, Seamus Finnegan decides to pull a boyish prank and turn a cup of water into rum. Whether this is a spell he had read somewhere or one of his own devising is unclear. What is clear is that rather than a cupful of rum, Seamus gets a face full of soot for his efforts.

Scabbers Gets Singed

DURING HARRY AND Ron's fateful first meeting on the train ride to Hogwarts in the *Harry Potter and the Sorcerer's Stone* film, Ron attempts to impress his new friend by showing him some of his magic skills. Waving his wand with a flourish, Ron recites what sounds like a rudimentary spell designed to turn his pet rat, Scabbers, yellow. Unfortunately, all he succeeds in doing is creating a small bit of combustion and some singed whiskers—in the book, Scabbers gets off easy, snoozing right through the spell entirely. Given that Scabbers eventually turns out to be Voldemort acolyte Peter Pettigrew in disguise, he probably had it coming.

Fred and George Grow Up Fast

IN *HARRY POTTER and the Goblet of Fire*, as preparations for the Triwizard Tournament get underway, Fred and George Weasley attempt to circumvent the tournament's age restriction spell with a little spell of their own. Drinking a potion that will seemingly conceal their real age, the twins step over the age line with confidence. At first, the spell seems to work perfectly. However, it quickly backfires, blasting the two away from the Goblet of Fire. When they sit up, they realize their spell has turned them into old men. So, technically, it worked, right?

Harry Gives His New Wand a Try

AFTER HIS OWN wand gets destroyed while on the run from Voldemort in *Harry Potter and the Deathly Hallows*, Harry is forced to fend with whatever he can get his hands on. Luckily, Ron is able to procure him a new, 10-inch wand he has stolen from a Snatcher. Eager to try it out, Harry points it at a candle and casts an engorging spell. Immediately, the candle roars to life, shooting a massive flame upwards to the ceiling of their tent. In shock, Harry quickly cries out "*Reducio!*" to bring the flame down, but not before Hermione inquires what Harry and Ron are up to.

THE FUNNIEST USES OF POLYJUICE POTION IN *HARRY POTTER*

HAVING THE ABILITY TO BECOME SOMEONE ELSE CAN BE USEFUL. IT CAN ALSO LEAD TO SOME COMEDY.

USING POLYJUICE POTION can be a tricky business. Apart from being a giant pain to brew, the slightest malfunction can mean disaster. (Just ask Hermione about her feline complications.) Even when it goes smoothly, however, using the potent potion has a way of producing comedic gold.

Harry and Ron Join Slytherin

IN *HARRY POTTER* *and the Chamber of Secrets,* Harry, Ron and Hermione brew up some of the shape-shifting concoction and try to infiltrate Slytherin House to gather information. Harry and Ron transform themselves into Goyle and Crabbe and use their disguises to gain access to the Slytherin common room. The pair trying to bluff their way through playing two of Hogwarts's biggest dimwits is funny enough, but the hilarity really ensues when Harry starts to transform back and Ron, as Crabbe, can barely stammer out "Scar!" to warn him.

"Moody" Transforms Malfoy

IN GENERAL, BARTY Crouch Jr.'s use of Polyjuice Potion isn't much to laugh about, but it did give us one standout moment of comedy: When Malfoy pulls his wand on Harry when his back is turned, Mad-Eye Moody (actually Crouch in a Polyjuice-assisted disguise) quickly intervenes, turning the hated Slytherin student into a ferret before using a wand to wave him around in the air. Professor McGonagall's horrified query of "Is that a student?" followed by Moody's response of, "Technically it's a ferret!" is amusing, but in hindsight, the fact that it's actually a Voldemort devotee doing the deed elevates the whole thing: Even Death Eaters hate Draco Malfoy.

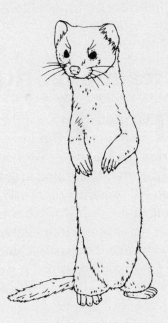

Ministers of Mischief

IN ORDER TO recover one of Voldemort's Horcruxes from the clutches of Dolores Umbridge at the Ministry of Magic, Harry, Ron and Hermione are forced to go undercover as Ministry employees to try to slip in and steal it. The three of them look and seem very much out of their element while in disguise, which leads to some comedic moments, including an uncomfortable elevator ride with Umbridge and Ron's heroic rescue of his "wife."

Hermione Hits Up the Bank

TRYING TO RECLAIM the sword of Gryffindor from the Lestrange vault at Gringotts, Hermione disguises herself as none other than one of the evilest witches in the magical world, Bellatrix Lestrange. These two couldn't be more different and it shows, as Hermione tries in vain to appear evil and demanding but still manages to come off as somewhat timid and polite.

Harrys, Harrys Everywhere

AS **A WAY** to confuse the Death Eaters in pursuit of Harry, members of the Order of the Phoenix decide to have Fred, George, Hermione, Ron, Mundugus Fletcher and Fleur Delacour drink Polyjuice to disguise themselves as Harry. They all have a bit of trouble adjusting to their new bodies, especially Fleur, who says "Look away, I'm hideous" to her husband, Bill.

Legends, Lore and History

PEER BACK THROUGH THE MISTS OF TIME
AND GET READY FOR SOME LEGENDARY LAUGHS!

What do you call a wizard storyteller who sings "All You Need is Love"?
BEATLE THE BARD.

★

What did the Irish wizard say when the Sorcerer's Stone didn't turn metal into gold?
"THIS IS A SHAM ROCK."

★

What happened when the Hogwarts founders broke off from Salazar Slytherin?
HE THREW A HISS-Y FIT.

★

Why did the wand decide to retire?
IT WAS AN ELDER WAND.

In "The Tale of the Three Brothers," what drink did the oldest brother offer Death when they finally met?
MORTALI-TEA.

★

What would Hagrid say to the bearded, long-haired warlock?
"YOU'RE A HAIRY WIZARD!"

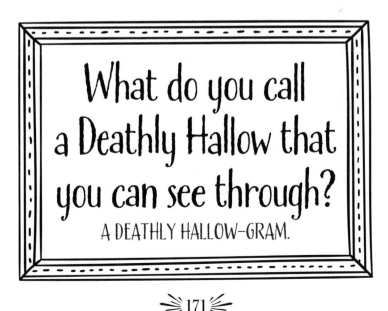

What do you call a Deathly Hallow that you can see through?
A DEATHLY HALLOW-GRAM.

What don't wizards want to find in their hot chocolate?
THE DEATHLY MALLOWS.

★

Where did Salazar Slytherin go to hear himself talk?
THE ECHO CHAMBER OF SECRETS.

★

Where did King Arthur buy animals to cross the desert with?
AT A CAMEL LOT.

★

Why did Godric Gryffindor always use a sword?
HE LOVED CUTTING-EDGE TECHNOLOGY.

Where did Gellert Grindelwald keep his armies?
IN HIS SLEEVIES.

★

Which knight built King Arthur's round table?
SIR CUMFERENCE.

How do we know Death was popular in the magical world?

PEOPLE WERE ALWAYS DYING TO MEET HIM.

What book did Beedle the Bard
write after getting badly burned?
The Tales of Beedle the Charred.

...and after getting
mauled by a Hippogriff?
The Tales of Beedle the Scarred.

...and after ending up in Azkaban?
The Tales of Beedle the Barred.

How did Babbity Rabbity get around?
BY HARE-PLANE.

How did Babbity Rabbity feel about
her plan to fool the king?
PRETTY HOP-TIMISTIC.

How did Babbity Rabbity feel
after fooling the king?
PRETTY HOPPY.

What do you call an alchemist who moves to Seattle and joins a grunge band?

NICOLAS FLANNEL.

What do you call a tabloid that bites your fingers when you try to read it?

THE NIBBLER.

★

What was the name of the knight who spied for Hogwarts?

SIR VEILLANCE.

★

What's Nicolas Flamel's favorite dog breed?

GOLDEN RETRIEVERS.

★

What does Nicolas Flamel like to eat?

KARAT CAKE.

Why would the Sword of Gryffindor do well on exams?

BECAUSE IT'S SO SHARP!

★

Why did the knight stop using an inflatable sword?

IT WAS POINTLESS.

How did Sir Cadogan know he could defeat a wyvern while riding his pony?
THEY HAD A STABLE RELATIONSHIP.

Did you hear Morrigan was almost sent to Azkaban for trying to meet with other wizards in her crow form?
SHE WAS CHARGED WITH ATTEMPTED MURDER.

★

Which legendary king also wrote books?
KING AUTHOR.

★

What happened when Celestina Warbeck couldn't find a singing partner?
SHE HAD TO GET A DUET YOURSELF KIT.

What happened when Hankerton Humble tried to contact Peeves to make peace?
HE KEPT GETTING GHOSTED.

Did you know Merlin had bad feet, a sensitive ego and terrible breath?

HE WAS A SUPER-CALLOUSED, FRAGILE WIZARD HEXED BY HALITOSIS.

Why did Ottaline Gambol decide to acquire a Muggle train and turn it into the Hogwarts Express?

SHE HAD A LOCO-MOTIVE.

★

What's the best way to carve a wand?

WHITTLE BY WHITTLE.

★

What did Angus Buchanan's family think when he left them to play rugby with Muggles?

THEY THOUGHT IT WAS A SCRUMMY THING TO DO.

I heard Helga Hufflepuff collected badgers.

SHE ALMOST HAD A FULL SETT.

**How did the Ollivanders
first arrive in Britain?**
THEY WAND-ERED OVER.

★

**Why does the Book of
Admittance hang out with
the Quill of Acceptance?**
THEY'RE PEN PALS.

★

**How did Celestina Warbeck get
locked out of her house?**
SHE HAD THE WRONG KEY.

★

**What do the Wizengamot
wear to work?**
LAWSUITS.

**Why was Ignatia
Wildsmith, inventor of
Floo Powder, so revered?**
NO ONE COULD HOLD A CANDLE
TO WHAT SHE MADE.

Why did the Durmstrang ship crash into the dock?

**THE DOCK WAS CLOSER
THAN IT A-PIER-ED.**

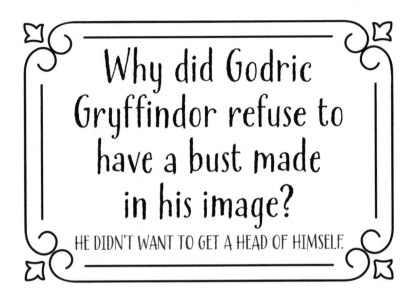

Why did Godric Gryffindor refuse to have a bust made in his image?

HE DIDN'T WANT TO GET A HEAD OF HIMSELF.

What did the Sorting Hat say to Godric Gryffindor?

"YOU STAY HERE, I'LL GO ON A HEAD."

★

What do you call a dinosaur that can cast spells?

A TYRANNOSAURUS HEX.

★

Was Nearly Headless Nick popular at Hogwarts?

HE WAS NEARLY HEAD BOY.

★

Did you hear about the Secret Keeper charged with protecting the recipe for an Indian bread?

HE HAD A NAAN DISCLOSURE AGREEMENT.

Have you heard about the famous wizard detective from the 1800s?

HIS NAME WAS WARLOCK HOLMES.

**Why could no one else pull
Excalibur from the stone?**
THEY DIDN'T HAVE ARTHURIZATION.

★

**What is it called when a wizard
gets robbed by a No-Maj?**
GETTING MUGGLED.

**What do you call a
blood-sucking insect who
reads *The Quibbler*?**
A LUNA-TICK.

★

**Why did Godric Gryffindor
put the Sorting Hat
on his knee?**
TO MAKE IT A KNEE CAP.

★

**Why should you
avoid the bank
in the Great Lake?**
IT'S FILLED WITH LOAN SHARKS.

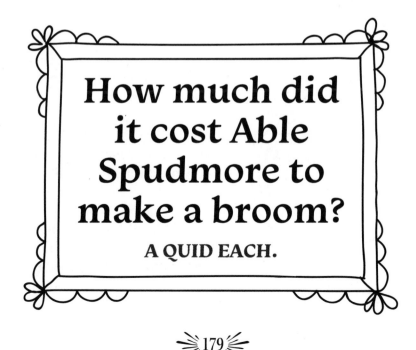

How much did it cost Able Spudmore to make a broom?

A QUID EACH.

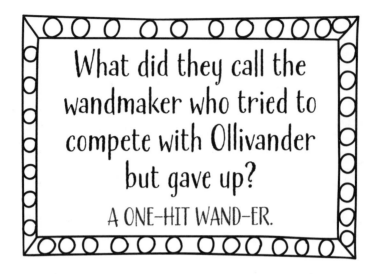

What did they call the wandmaker who tried to compete with Ollivander but gave up?

A ONE-HIT WAND-ER.

Did Quidditch become popular after the first World Cup?

IT SWEPT THE GLOBE.

What's in the toilet in the Chamber of Secrets?

TOM RIDDLE'S DIARRHEA.

★

What do you call a parent-teacher conference held under an Invisibility Cloak?

A TRANSPARENT-TEACHER CONFERENCE.

★

What's the only thing the worst player at the first Quidditch World Cup caught?

A COLD!

★

Why did the Dumbledore bring his writing tablet in the shower every morning?

HE WANTED TO START EACH DAY WITH A CLEAN SLATE.

A woman is brought before the judge in the Salem Witch Trials. "You have been accused of doing dark magic, witch!" the judge says. "It's misdirection," says the woman. "Fine," says the judge. "You have been accused of doing dark magic, **Miss Direction!**"

What did Salazar Slytherin give the Basilisk before leaving it in the Chamber of Secrets?
A GOODNIGHT HISS.

★

Did you hear about the Hidebehind who tried to shapeshift into an owl?
HE BECAME A WHO-MAN BEING!

★

What did Marlowe Forfang call a sleeping werewolf?
AN UNAWARE WOLF.

★

What happened to Able Spudmore when a test of the Firebolt went wrong?
HE HAD A BRUSH WITH DEATH.

What do you get when you mix three magical objects with the King of Rock & Roll?
THE PRESLEY HALLOWS.

★

Why couldn't you trust Voldemort's diary?
IT WAS RIDDLED WITH LIES.

If Salazar Slytherin were still alive today, what would he be famous for?

HIS AGE.

Why did the wizard lose his job tracking Death Eaters at the Ministry of Magic?

HE WAS AUROR-BLE AT IT.

Who did the judges call at the Salem Witch Trials for evidence?
WITCH-NESSES.

Why did the Quidditch player get banned from the first World Cup?
FOR SWEEPING ON THE JOB.

★

Why did the cow need an invisibility cloak?
FOR CA-MOO-FLAGE.

★

How did Moaning Myrtle feel when she first saw Harry?
A LITTLE FLUSHED.

★

Why can't you take the Knight Bus to Hogwarts?
IT WON'T FIT THROUGH THE DOOR!

Why was the Minister of Magic at IKEA?

HE WAS TRYING TO GET HIS CABINET TOGETHER.

★

Why are vampires rarely seen in the magical world?

EVERYONE THINKS THEY'RE A PAIN IN THE NECK.

★

Why is rain over Hogwarts like the Battle of Hogwarts?

BOTH INVOLVE STORMING THE CASTLE.

★

Did the first Knight Bus run on time?

NO, IT RAN ON WHEELS.

What's the first thing a wizard does every morning?

WAKE UP.

★

Why do vampires read *The Daily Prophet*?

IT HAS GOOD CIRCULATION.

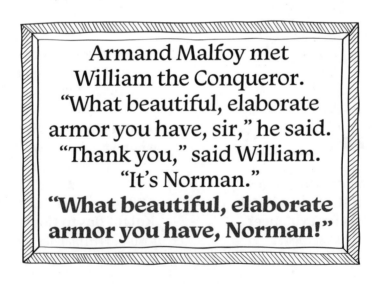

Armand Malfoy met William the Conqueror. "What beautiful, elaborate armor you have, sir," he said. "Thank you," said William. "It's Norman." **"What beautiful, elaborate armor you have, Norman!"**

KNOCK KNOCK.
Who's there?
Familiar.
Familiar who?
**This house is Familiar.
Do I live here?**

KNOCK KNOCK.
Who's there?
MACUSA.
MACUSA who?
**MACUSA you of
locking me out!**

KNOCK KNOCK.
Who's there?
Sasquatch.
Sasquatch who?
**Sasquatch me break
down this door!**

KNOCK KNOCK.
Who's there?
Dragot.
Dragot who?
**Let's not Dragot
this conversation.
Let me in!**

KNOCK KNOCK.
Who's there?
No-Maj.
No-Maj who?
**No-Maj-er what,
I am coming in!**

KNOCK KNOCK.
Who's there?
Seer
Seer who?
**Can you Seer way
to opening
the door?**

KNOCK KNOCK.
Who's there?
Erised.
Erised who?
**Eri-sed to open
the door!**

KNOCK KNOCK.
Who's there?
Kettleburn.
Kettleburn who?
**Kettleburn
my tongue!**

How do the ghosts feel about Hogwarts?

THAT IT'S HAUNTED BY PEOPLE.

What was the reaction to Lyall Lupin's book about poltergeists?

COPIES WERE FLYING OFF SHELVES.

★

What happened when Rancorous Carpe tried to exorcise Peeves from Hogwarts?

THE SCHOOL GOT RE-POSSESSED.

★

Why did Vindictus Viridian say depressing things to his blackberry potion?

TO TRY AND TURN IT INTO A BLUEBERRY POTION.

How did Silvanus Kettleburn weigh his dragons?

LUCKILY, THEY CAME WITH SCALES.

Linfred of
Stinchcombe
treated a wizard for
a difficult ailment.
"Thank you so
much!" the wizard
said. "How can
I ever repay your
kindness?"
"I take Sickles,
Knuts and
Galleons..."

Acknowledgments

I HAVE BEEN A fan of the *Harry Potter* series since I first read the books to my kids when they were little, straining my voice into the best Hagrid impression I could muster. As such, this project was a fun undertaking, delving into the sillier side of the magical world. I have to thank the incredible team at Media Lab Books for their support and guidance on this book, especially Tony Romando, Jeff Ashworth, Tim Baker, Courtney Kerrigan and Phil Sexton. And continued thanks must always go to my family, Alli, William and James. I'm glad you can still laugh at my jokes and am grateful for all the smiles you bring me in return.

About the Author

JEREMY K. BROWN has written about pop culture and entertainment for various websites and print publications for 20 years. He is the author of *The Official John Wayne Big Book of Dad Jokes* and *The WWE Championship: The Greatest Title in Sports Entertainment*. He is also the author of the science fiction novels *Ocean of Storms* (with Christopher Mari) and *Zero Limit*. A proud Gryffindor, he does a mean Hagrid impression and, much like Dobby, has received socks as a gift on more than one occasion.

Media Lab Books
For inquiries, call 646-449-8614

Copyright 2023 Jeremy Brown

Published by Topix Media Lab
14 Wall Street, Suite 3C
New York, NY 10005

Printed in China

ISBN-13: 978-1-956403-38-1
ISBN-10: 1-956403-38-8

CEO Tony Romando

Vice President & Publisher Phil Sexton
Senior Vice President of Sales & New Markets Tom Mifsud
Vice President of Retail Sales & Logistics Linda Greenblatt
Chief Financial Officer Vandana Patel
Manufacturing Director Nancy Puskuldjian
Digital Marketing & Strategy Manager Elyse Gregov

Chief Content Officer Jeff Ashworth
Director of Editorial Operations Courtney Kerrigan
Senior Acquisitions Editor Noreen Henson
Creative Director Susan Dazzo
Photo Director Dave Weiss
Managing Editor Tara Sherman

Content Editor Tim Baker
Content Designer Alyssa Bredin Quirós
Features Editor Trevor Courneen
Associate Editor Juliana Sharaf
Designers Glen Karpowich, Mikio Sakai
Copy Editor & Fact Checker Madeline Raynor
Assistant Photo Editor Jenna Addesso

Cover art and all interior art: Shutterstock